CHAMPIONS!

CHAMPIONS!
HOW THE WORLD CUP WAS WON

Suresh Menon

First Published in 2011 by Harper Sport
An imprint of HarperCollins *Publishers*
a joint venture with
The India Today Group

Text copyright © Suresh Menon 2011
Photographs copyright © Getty Images 2011

ISBN: 978-93-5029-156-6

2 4 6 8 10 9 7 5 3 1

Suresh Menon asserts the moral right to be identified
as the author of this work.

All rights reserved. No part of this publication may be reproduced,
stored in a retrieval system, or transmitted, in any form or by any means,
electronic, mechanical, photocopying, recording or otherwise,
without the prior permission of the publishers.

HarperCollins *Publishers*
A-53, Sector 57, NOIDA, Uttar Pradesh - 201301, India
77-85 Fulham Palace Road, London W6 8JB, United Kingdom
Hazelton Lanes, 55 Avenue Road, Suite 2900, Toronto, Ontario M5R 3L2
and 1995 Markham Road, Scarborough, Ontario M1B 5M8, Canada
25 Ryde Road, Pymble, Sydney, NSW 2073, Australia
31 View Road, Glenfield, Auckland 10, New Zealand
10 East 53rd Street, New York NY 10022, USA

Art Director **Shuka Jain**
Designer **Anuj Malhotra**

Printed and bound by
Nutech Print Services

To my late father, the quintessential fan, who watched the inaugural match but was gone before the India-England tie. His last words: 'No regrets'.

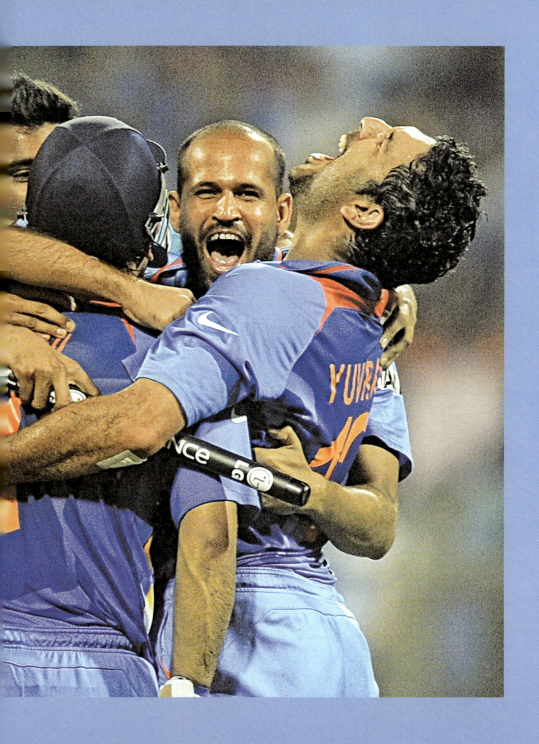

CONTENTS

1. Dhoni Did It His Way — 01
2. The End Of Anxiety — 15
3. Where It Began — 23
4. Y And Z And The X-Factor — 31
5. The Quiet Motivator — 41
6. A Tournament Of Two Halves — 49
7. Living Up To Expectations — 59
8. A Call For Magnanimity — 75
9. An All-time India XI — 87

Scorecards — 95

Acknowledgements — 148

Dhoni Did It His Way

The inevitability of India's win, the influence of Dhoni and other factors

In the end, it boiled down to the look in skipper Mahendra Singh Dhoni's eyes as he struck Nuwan Kulasekera for a six to claim the World Cup for India. Television captured the fire in his eyes in a telling close-up. That picture had everything.

As in great poetry, there were layers of meaning in that expression, and stories that could be written separately about each emotion so nakedly present—the focus, the pride, the sheer joy, the self-confidence, relief at the conclusion, relief at having done it his way an=d succeeded, and much more. Powerful human emotions, but there was, too, something almost non-human in that look.

Should all the records of the 2011 World Cup be somehow lost or forgotten, the history of the tournament can be reconstructed from that one look alone.

World Cups are won by captains. Think Clive Lloyd 1975, Kapil Dev 1983, Allan Border 1987, Imran Khan 1992, Arjuna Ranatunga 1996, Ricky Ponting 2003. M.S. Dhoni 2011 is a worthy addition to that list.

The shorter the game, the more important is the ability to make quick decisions, and the greater the impact of such decisions. An unexpected bowling change, a minor adjustment in the field that leads to a catch or a run out, a sudden decision to keep down runs for five overs before going on the attack—such things can turn a game. Little things matter, and it is the captain who controls the little things. Dhoni controlled them well, especially in the latter part of the tournament.

Captain Cool is also Captain Ruthless, Captain Pragmatic, Captain A-historical, Captain No-nonsense. Dhoni seems unburdened by history, his mind uncluttered by might-have-beens. He is simple without being simplistic, straightforward without being naive, and above all, he knows his

01

CHAMPIONS!

own mind with an intimacy denied to most. His decisiveness comes from trusting his instincts, his confidence from an almost childlike certainty that ultimately everything will turn out right. He is the calm in the eye of the storm.

His players look up to him. 'I want a team,' he once said, 'that can stand before a truck.' He had just such a team, and his contribution to building it was crucial.

Sachin Tendulkar said he is the finest captain he has played under; for Praveen Kumar, the medium pacer who was injured before the World Cup, Dhoni is the Obama of cricket.

Dhoni thought he had won the toss in the final, but was willing to have it re-taken since the match referee didn't hear the call. Under pressure and with the eyes of the world on him, Dhoni made the right gesture; after all, India were the hosts, and the Indian captain had to be hospitable.

In any case, Dhoni was determined to turn received wisdom on its head. No host team had won the Cup; no team had won chasing; no team had won after an opponent had made a century. But before the feast, there was the reckoning. There was the equally cool, equally determined Mahela Jayawardene, that most elegant of right-handers, standing in the way.

In an era of bats that can casually mishit for six and innovations named after the mongoose, Jayawardene is a throwback to another generation. He is a modern with the heart of a golden-age hero. No contemporary bats with such soft hands. This, allied to his quick feet and cricketing intelligence, makes him a modern great.

Jayawardene's 88-ball 103 invited comparison with the century made in the 1996 final by the batsman he is most often bracketed with, Aravinda de Silva. Both men run the gamut from delicate touch to ferocious pulls; both men are big-event performers, reserving their best for the times when their team is in trouble and batting authority the crying need. Both men change gears with startling frequency. Aravinda could be brutal, but that is not a word associated with Jayawardene, who can destroy bowlers with a smile and a late cut played so late the fielder at third man is already preparing for the next delivery!

It is this delicacy of touch, this exquisite sense of timing, this ability to preserve the image of the entire field in his mind's eye and hit into the gaps that makes Jayawardene special. When he was captain, he urged his players to express their uniqueness. 'Our strength is our flair, and we must exploit this,' he said. 'We should not play like Australia, England or India. We should play like Sri Lanka.' It is a philosophy that defines the Sri Lankan cricket team today.

At 60 for two in the 17th over, the match was India's. Jayawardene refused to accept that, and before you knew it, he was in his 80s. It was a silent march, the ball hitting the middle of the bat and speeding away as if embarrassed to be seen to be making a fuss. He had saved the best innings of the tournament for the final match. It meant Sri Lanka made 274, and India would have to score more than any other team to win a final. It might have exceeded 300 but for a third outstanding day in the field for the Indians, who throughout the early phase of the tournament had seemed to be fielding under protest.

The World Cup final was also about defiance in defeat. Here, Mahela Jayawardene exults after scoring one of the finest centuries in the tournament.

The inner circle of Yuvraj Singh, Suresh Raina and Virat Kohli was spectacular. When Indians throw themselves around it is a special day, and when they field like this, it is a hint that something incredible is about to happen.

Still, at 31 for two, India had a hill to climb. But this day had been approached with a lot of thought and much preparation. The bowlers had done their job, the fielders had exceeded their brief, and now it was up to India's strength, the batting, to deliver.

At no point did India struggle. Gautam Gambhir's discipline saw him in two vital partnerships, with Kohli and then with his skipper. Neither he nor Dhoni had really played to potential till the final, but that didn't matter. Dhoni promoting himself above Yuvraj spoke of his instinct and his cricketing nous. It was the captain leading from the front. The right-left combination was an effort to thwart the Sri Lankan off-spinners. And Dhoni could bat with some freedom, knowing the man in form was yet to come in. As with so many moves the captain had made throughout his career, the romantic and the pragmatic were in perfect blend. More importantly, it worked, and Dhoni, already a demigod in a nation constantly searching to add to its long list, earned a promotion in the hierarchy of gods.

He did it his way. He picked the players he wanted, managed the difficult task of keeping them match-fit and motivated through six weeks, ignored the criticism from the media and former players, ensured that the weakest links contributed, publicized how the players took care of one another regardless of who was in or out of the team, and above all, saw the team peak at the right time. This meant they played their best cricket in the final match. That final six seemed to focus all these diverse elements in one moment.

It wasn't easy. Through much of the tournament Dhoni alone seemed to understand what the plan was. Just because you don't see a pattern it doesn't mean there isn't one, he might have shouted at the media, which appeared more confused than the match referee. But that would have been rude, and Dhoni was magnanimous in victory. It wasn't about proving others wrong so much as proving himself right.

Had India lost, all the stock criticisms would have been given another airing: the terrible fielding, the inconsistent team selection, the refusal to experiment in inconsequential games, the confidence placed in some players to the exclusion of others, a refusal to attack at crucial phases, and more.

CHAMPIONS!

But victory is a solvent in which all criticisms disappear.

If anyone had said in the group phase that India's fielding would make the difference, they would have been stating the obvious. But in a negative sense. Yet here was Yuvraj Singh throwing himself around with the attitude of a teenager trying to impress his girlfriend. Even Zaheer Khan, who tended to maintain a distant relationship with the speeding ball, was now attacking it with vigour. India saved 25-30 runs in the final, and that made the difference.

Where did that energy come from? When did a bunch of players who were driving their supporters and even their captain to distraction, suddenly decide to raise the tone of their fielding? 'You can't do anything about our fielding. It is not going to improve,' Dhoni had said repeatedly. For once, he was wrong. The improvement began with the quarterfinal against Australia when Raina came into the team. That immediately doubled the number of good fielders in the side—Kohli having played a lone hand till then. But it was the reawakening of the others that was remarkable. Sri Lanka, a superior fielding outfit till then, now looked ragged. India's transformation had shocked them into exploring their inefficient side.

Perhaps the overemphasis on Sachin Tendulkar's century of centuries had enabled the bowlers and fielders to work on their skills away from public attention. If so, that was another, unheralded contribution by the Little Master.

Sri Lanka's relatively smoother passage into the final worked against them. There was no wriggling out of tight situations, no dramatic final-moment win, no match that tested their staying power or strategy for handling pressure. India, in contrast, sleepwalked through the league phase, were threatened even by Ireland, and so by the time they reached the final they had been tested, wrung out and dried in different situations.

Was this the finest World Cup ever?

Just as the tournament put the stamp on Asian resurgence, it brought to an end the domination of Australia, who had won the last three championships. Ricky Ponting bowed out with one of the most courageous centuries in one-day cricket, standing tall as everyone around him fell, and ignoring both a fractured finger and calls for his head. The journey had begun for Australia in the 1987 World Cup in the subcontinent, so things had come full circle.

Other teams lived up to the clichés around them. South Africa choked again, twice. Pakistan oscillated between brilliance and silliness, New Zealand were good enough to get to the semifinals but not further, England were inconsistent, losing to Bangladesh and Ireland but beating South Africa and the West Indies. And the West Indies, who once strutted like champions, continued to be in terminal decline, with players displaying little pride in their work.

Quite the remarkable thing about India's World Cup was what came after. For once, victory was not followed by hysteria, although all manner of politicians did jump on the bandwagon and announce all manner of awards, from land to cash and unto half the kingdom they had no authority over anyway. But that is what we expect from our politicians, and there would have been great disappointment if they hadn't sought the limelight thus.

No, what was remarkable was the business-as-usual attitude. The players changed into even more colourful clothing (suggesting that the more colours you wear, the lower the grade of cricket, from Tests to one-dayers to T20), and took guard at the IPL, pausing along the way only long enough to shave a head or pay obeisance to assorted gurus.

The fans, too, took guard at the IPL, if you go by one of the many names given to Anna Hazare's movement against corruption. This one, called 'Indian People's League', had the same demographic as those who cheered India's progress through the World Cup. Although logicians talk about the danger of assuming that 'B' is caused by 'A' simply because B follows A, there is something about the timing, the effervescence of the Citizens Against Corruption movement that seemed to suggest it was riding on the feel-good factor generated by the World Cup win.

Recent research has indicated that the feel-good factor gives the economy a boost; it has also indicated that the effect is negligible. Yet the concept is so attractive that England's 1966 World Cup soccer win was credited with the landslide re-election of Harold Wilson as prime minister—although the elections took place three whole months before the soccer final!

To say that Dhoni batting in Mumbai influenced the Gandhian Anna Hazare fasting for a cause in Delhi might be far-fetched. But what cannot be denied is that sporting success makes people feel

Flags with the portraits of cricketers on them, replicas of the World Cup, laughter, chants and bonhomie lit up celebrations around the country. Many of the revellers were not even born when India last won the title, and this was an opportunity to associate with sporting history.

CHAMPIONS!

more optimistic. Germany knew this in 1936 and Argentina in 1978, when they won the soccer World Cup. Some sports work better than others in creating this sense of national well-being; nothing works like cricket in India.

The poet Gerard Manley Hopkins has said that the springs of sorrow are the same; perhaps so, too, are the springs of joy. It is possible to imagine the confidence and increased self-worth that comes from a sporting success being translated into a movement against exploitation. The power that comes from victory is the opposite of the powerlessness in the face of government corruption and a system that has to be endured because the alternative is too horrible to contemplate.

Other things have to fall into place too. After all, the Lokpal bill is some four decades old, and it might be argued that Kapil Dev's winners of 1983 had the same opportunity to inspire a nation. Let us just say the climate was right, and Dhoni's victory was not unhelpful.

DHONI DID IT HIS WAY

A new benchmark

This was a tournament that was necessary to restore faith in a World Cup that had floundered in the West Indies four years ago, easily one of the most poorly organized of the ten editions so far. The average fan struggled to watch a match as much due to the high price of tickets as to the various do's and don'ts he was subjected to. Stands were often empty. In the subcontinent, by contrast, there were healthy crowds even for the minor games, and Bangladesh in particular brought to the grounds a spectacular mix of excitement and sheer energy.

There were complaints from various centres in India that the public—now called 'civil society', thanks to the anti-corruption movement—was denied access to tickets thanks to an outmoded system of patronage, the greed of the local politicians and bureaucrats, and the corruption among the officials. You either got the tickets early or had to wait till an unshaven, often flag-bearing tout called out his wares thus: 'Flag, flag, black, black, flag, black…' The cooperation between the cop and the criminal in this endeavour might have been touching in another time and place.

Yet 2011 is the new benchmark. It was the best World Cup played, even if the quality of some of the matches wasn't inspiring. An amazing tie in the India-England encounter early on hinted at the possibilities, but in the end both the semifinals were disappointing, cricket-wise.

Closing a chapter

Kapil Dev holding up the World Cup in 1983 is one of Indian sport's iconic images. At the other end of the emotional scale is the most telling picture of the 2007 World Cup—India's senior batsmen looking devastated.

There's skipper Rahul Dravid, hand on face covering one eye, possibly wiping away a tear. Sachin Tendulkar sits to his left, hand over mouth, in intense shock. Behind them is Virender Sehwag, face cupped in hand. In each case the eyes tell the story. A combination of disbelief, personal loss, shame, ruin, disillusionment, horror and self-pity.

'I cried then, I cried now, but this time they were tears of joy,' said Tendulkar. The sight of one of the great batsmen blubbering at the end of an exhausting tournament suggested just how much it meant

CHAMPIONS!

The first time... Kapil Dev with the 1983 World Cup

in his 22nd year of international cricket. Tendulkar might not have notched up his one hundredth century—the biggest non-event of the World Cup—but that will come with time. This, meanwhile, was his sixth and possibly last chance to get his hands on the trophy, and he had played a significant role in getting India there.

Sport is about upsets, it is also about the inevitable coming to pass and leaving fans with the feeling that god's in his heaven and all's right with the world. The two best teams met in the final and the better team won.

India breathed new life not only into the World Cup, which had begun to look like an exclusive Australian preserve since 1999, they revived the format itself. The 50-over game, threatened by the glitz and money of T20, had been in danger of being forgotten if the World Cup had gone wrong (and, let's face it, if India had not won).

For his runs and wickets, Yuvraj Singh was the Player of the Tournament, but the player with the biggest impact on it was skipper Dhoni. He took the pressure, took the criticism, took the defeat against South Africa with a maturity and understanding that was other-worldly. He had the weakest bowling combination of all the semifinalists and the weakest fielding side when the tournament began. Yet he moulded the combination into a unit that played above itself.

On spin-friendly wickets, medium pacer Zaheer Khan was the star; after runs had leaked through porous fields in the league, the team suddenly got a grip, and sparkled in the final. Dhoni and coach Gary Kirsten had got the timing right—the team peaked when it mattered.

Asked about future ambitions, Dhoni said simply, 'I don't mind repeating everything.'

More to the point, Dhoni saw the World Cup as having 'ended a chapter', in which detail it was different from the 1983 triumph, which was the start of a chapter. Less than half the team will survive till the next World Cup. Sehwag, Zaheer and Nehra will be 36 and Harbhajan 34. India will have to find fresh young batsmen (with the likes of Kohli, Raina, Yuvraj and Gambhir, who will be only 33 four years from now, acting as the bridge between generations). A new set of medium pacers will have to come through too.

The chapter that was ending was opened with the T20 win of 2007, according to Dhoni. 'Right now we can close the chapter,' he said after the final. 'We need to build a team again. Because of the amount of cricket we play, we need quite a few reserve players to come in and bowl. We need spinners and batsmen to be at their best because if we want to do well at the international level, we will have to try out quite a few players and not think about the result.' The cycle of birth, death, rebirth is as germane to international sport as it is to the Hindu way of life.

The End Of Anxiety

2

The psychological impact on cricket-watching in India, for so long moored to anxiety and uncertainty

Lord's Test, 1971. India, fresh from a series victory in the West Indies, had taken the first innings lead over England. Now they needed 38 runs to win, with two wickets remaining, including that of the man in form, Eknath Solkar. I can't remember who the commentator was, it might have been John Arlott. He informed those of us sitting around a Murphy radio at home in Bangalore that it had begun to rain. Thousands across the country must have done what we children then did—we broke into a rain dance, to encourage the gods further.

It worked. The match was washed out. The newspapers carried a cartoon of a local driver refusing to drive a bus in London because it was No. 38. We thought it was hilarious. We revelled in the glow of defeat averted. Not to lose was the greatest victory then.

Years later I discovered that the reaction in the Indian dressing room had not been very different. Skipper Ajit Wadekar didn't break into a dance, but he blessed the rain, and the mood in the dressing room turned upbeat. It was taken for granted—by the players, the media, the fans—that India would not have made it.

Four decades later, the psychological turnaround is complete. At 31 for two in the final of the World Cup, and with India's best batsmen dismissed, only the generation that had followed the Lord's Test of 1971 had any doubts. We were prepared for the worst—another Vijay Amritraj moment in sport. The cliché was near at hand, had always been: so near and yet so far. Amritraj, once considered more talented than his contemporaries Bjorn Borg and Jimmy Connors, was always magnificent in defeat. But mainly it was defeat. Talent that didn't go all the way, the story of Indian sport.

This time, however, it was different. The radio had given way to television, and the group around it was not unlike the group around the radio all those years ago. But the atmosphere was different.

A picture of balance... Sunil Gavaskar shows how it can be done in a skull cap.

CHAMPIONS!

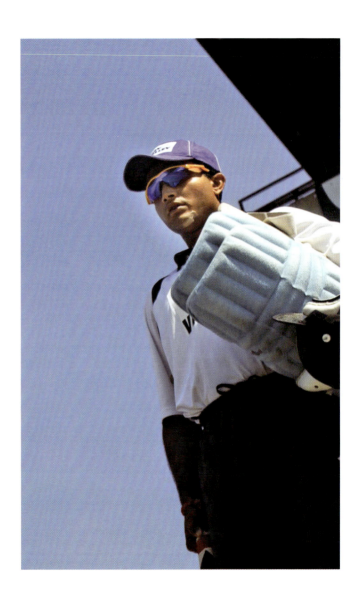

Sourav Ganguly came closest to matching Kapil Dev's achievement when he led India into the final of the 2003 World Cup. That was 20 years later, and already fans were feeling the wait had been too long.

THE END OF ANXIETY

The younger ones didn't flinch. My son leaned over and bet the price of a Dream Theater CD that India would not only win, but win easily. He is a fan in the age of Tendulkar—confident, self-assured, and with faith in the cricket team. A completely different animal from his father, who is wracked by uncertainty and carries too many memories of promise collapsing at the last hurdle.

Has an era finally ended? The era of Doubting Thomases and The-other-team-will-win Certainties? The era when the dominant emotion at an India match was not anticipation but anxiety, and everyone believed that even if India had to score ten runs in ten overs with ten wickets in hand, they would somehow manage to screw it up?

When Virender Sehwag says today that he always backs the opposition, he means it as a joke, as a way of proving to himself the sheer absurdity of such thinking. Not so long ago, that was the way to bet. When India made their Test debut in 1932, they reduced England to 19 for three in the first half hour of play. Then, shocked at their own impertinence, they allowed England back into the game, to lose by 158 runs. For the first 20 years—while a whole generation came and went—India didn't have a single victory. The C.K. Nayudus, Mohammed Nissars, Amar Singhs, Vijay Merchants rocked the world as individuals but Team India had nothing to show for it.

National ambitions were moored to simplicity. The prayers were practical: 'Please god, let Merchant score a 50' or 'Let CK hit a couple of sixes'. Fifty scored, sixes hit, the fans were happy. Indians were not expected to win anything, their aim was to be honourable in defeat. Sometimes even that was a tall order. One summer in Manchester, Fred Trueman and Alec Bedser combined to dismiss India twice in a day for 58 and 98. Not much honour in that.

It was only when a genius named Sunil Gavaskar appeared that we began to fantasize about drawing matches we would earlier have lost easily.

We are now in Phase 3—the Tendulkar phase, although Sourav Ganguly must be given credit too, for leading India to a string of victories abroad.

We have become a nation that believes. The anxiety has been replaced by belief, the worst-case scenario is merely a reduction in the margin of victory. We lose now and then, of course, but there is no inevitability about it. India began as favourites and won the World Cup. Now, in close finishes, the intelligent money will be on India.

CHAMPIONS!

The 1983 win showed that 'we can win'; this one, that 'we must win'.

India won only 23 Tests of the 125 that Gavaskar played, but they drew 68, or 54 per cent. Even in one-day internationals, despite the resurgence in the years around the 1983 World Cup win, India still lost more games than they won of Gavaskar's 108.

Tendulkar changed all that. His win-loss record in Tests is 61-46 and in ODIs 230-195. A whole generation with more points on the credit side has grown up around him.

Mahendra Singh Dhoni has confessed that he didn't watch the 2003 World Cup final. 'I switched off the TV when Tendulkar got out,' he explained. If watching Tendulkar bat is a national obsession, switching off the TV when he got out had become a national habit. Till now. He was dismissed cheaply in the final, but there was no panic either in living rooms across the country or in the home dressing room in Mumbai.

India have traversed the path from valour in defeat to honourable draw to inevitable victory. Youngsters assume victory is a natural corollary of being Indian. The 2003 team that lost in the final may have been a better team than the one that won this year. But neither the players nor the fans had crossed this important psychological barrier.

The beginning of belief

Cricket fandom in India has traditionally been fraught with stress, tension and foreboding. Would Gavaskar, the greatest run-maker of the era, score a century in the same match in which the greatest match-winner, B.S. Chandrasekhar, claimed five wickets in an innings? That happened just thrice.

Hence the private arrangements with the cricketing gods. About turning vegetarian, about shaving off hair, about donating to temples, about not using foul language for a week. Simple, doable things.

THE END OF ANXIETY

No one promised to take off all their clothes and parade around in the stadium, as a model did in 2011 (before deciding that keeping clothes on was the better part of valour).

This latter is not fandom, merely publicity-seeking, and that's a whole different genre. It is the bandwagon effect that makes prime ministers, politicians, movie actors, models all pretend to love the game and want to contribute to it with their humble presence, fully clothed or otherwise.

The fan who watched the final without making a single visit to the toilet sacrificed more. 'This is the least I could do for my country,' he said proudly (but softly, in case it set off something he couldn't

CHAMPIONS!

control). It meant he didn't miss a single minute of the action—or a single commercial. And since the Indian skipper was seen most often in both, this fan is a bit uncertain about whether India actually won or what he saw was a commercial. Strong bladders can lead to weak minds sometimes.

Just as cricket has undergone a change, so too has fandom. This has been said often enough, but bears repetition—Indians are fans not so much of cricket as of cricketers. You only have to see the attendance at a Ranji Trophy match to understand this. Three men and a dog make up the audience, and sometimes one of them takes the dog for a walk and the crowd is abruptly reduced by fifty per cent.

In the days when Gundappa Vishwanath was rewriting the geometry of batsmanship, crowds flocked to watch him in local league matches. On one occasion, I borrowed a bicycle and rode a great distance to see him play in a tennis-ball match. Turned out he was the chief guest and didn't actually play, but it didn't matter.

Fans had no guarantees then; the uncertainty was often devastating. You might walk on the road avoiding all the cracks in the pavement or make sure you touched every electric pole on the way to the stadium or bribe the gods in a hundred different ways. But you knew in your heart that you—and India—were fighting a losing battle.

Tendulkar, and now Dhoni, have changed all that. From anxiety to belief in three steps spread over several decades. The bladder controller can let go at the next World Cup, and the model can keep her clothes on. It doesn't mean that India will win everything from here on. Just that long-suffering fans will not need to make so many sacrifices.

Where It Began

The start of the journey which ended in Mumbai. Also 1987 and 1996

How far back do you go? To Australia three years before the World Cup and the picture of a smiling Dhoni after India had beaten the hosts in the final of the Commonwealth Bank series and the skipper's gamble of opening the bowling with Praveen Kumar had paid off?

Or to the 2007 T20 world championship where an earlier gamble, bringing on Joginder Sharma to bowl the last, over in the final, had paid off and India changed the face of world cricket with their triumph?

Or further back, to 2006 and Rahul Dravid's feat of leading an Indian team through nine consecutive one-day victories against Pakistan and England?

Or to Sourav Ganguly bare-chested on the Lord's balcony, waving his shirt above his head after India had beaten England in the Natwest final in 2002, coming back from a hopeless position thanks partly to the man who, nearly nine years later, would be the Player of the Tournament at the 2011 World Cup?

We can keep going backwards, to 1987 and 1996, when the World Cup was held in the subcontinent and India lost both times in the semifinals. Or to 1983 and India's first World Cup win under Kapil Dev, or 1974 when India made their one-day debut, nose in the air and treating the new format as an unnecessary evil.

'We saw the one-day game merely as a contraction of Test cricket,' said India's first ODI captain Ajit Wadekar. 'We didn't take the game seriously.'

Both in 1987 and in 1996, India lost in the semifinals. Both times the captains might have erred in

CHAMPIONS!

choosing to field first on winning the toss; both times the captains threw their wickets away, adding to the pressure. Both times the Indian batsmen displayed a strange obsession with playing the sweep.

Both times the rival captains, England's Mike Gatting and Sri Lanka's Arjuna Ranatunga, confessed it might have been a good toss to lose. In 1987, opener Graham Gooch (who scored a century) said he would have batted first despite the description of Wankhede Stadium as a 'giant Turkish bath'.

India probably paid the price in two matches nine years apart, for playing not to their strengths but to the opponents' weaknesses. A Kapil Dev with greater confidence in his batsmen might have chosen to take first strike, to give his spinners Ravi Shastri and Maninder Singh something to bowl at.

Azharuddin claimed after the defeat at the Eden Gardens that it had been a 'collective decision'. He had Anil Kumble and offie Ashish Kapoor (to counter all those left-handers) in his side.

But we needn't go that far back. A mere 18 months will do, as skipper Dhoni said after the final. 'About one-and-a-half years

WHERE IT BEGAN

ago, we had set our eyes on the World Cup. Whatever we were doing on the field, we had a long-term goal to do well in the World Cup,' he said. 'We peaked at the right time and carried that momentum into the final.'

But Dhoni had the wider vision too. 'It started with the 1983 win. And two big players, Sachin Tendulkar and Anil Kumble, came on the scene, followed by Sourav Ganguly and Rahul Dravid,' he said, generously sharing the credit.

Preparation meant that players were rested and rotated, experiments were tried, and both the injured and those out of form were given opportunities to get back into full fitness and top of their form. Dhoni himself missed two series; Tendulkar did not play for nearly a year.

Of the 11 matches India played till the start of the World Cup, they won eight, including all six that were played at home. The losses came in a single series in South Africa.

Still, there is something to be said for the topless Ganguly celebration as the starting point. Although the 1983 achievement is kept alive by the media, and the players have microphones thrust at them and cameras at their elbows once every four years, 28 years is a long time in sport. You might be inspired in an abstract manner but it is too much like a story in India's many mythological tales for it to be real. Tendulkar was ten years old then, and remembers being struck by the success of Kapil Dev's men, but most of the others were either not yet born or still at the nappy-wearing stage.

25

Anil Kumble seems to have grown an extra hand to destroy the opposition. Wicketkeeper M.S.Dhoni, who succeeded him as India's captain, doesn't seem surprised at this development!

Like the Salt March or the adventures of the Rani of Jhansi, the 1983 triumph had moved from a tale of national heroism to dry statistics in a history textbook. And the endless replays of Madan Lal dismissing Viv Richards or players talking about team spirit had begun to pale. There is something pathetic about clinging to one hour of crowded glory in an age without a name. It will be interesting to see how Dhoni's victory will be treated in the next decade or the one after that.

The 2003 final was more real, and some of the youngsters in the current team had actually watched the game. If 2003 was a positive influence, so too was 2007, when India failed to make the knockout. The national mourning that followed must have strengthened the resolve of the players to make up for that disaster. Tendulkar admitted as much after the 2011 final. He had to get that monkey off his back, and not just he, players like Sehwag and Zaheer and Yuvraj too, men who turned out to be the heroes of India's win.

Ganguly had led India into the 2003 final a year after the Natwest celebration on the Lord's balcony. That win was unexpected, and seen as a bonus. But what was not so readily appreciated was the fact that Ganguly was responsible for a second self-respect movement in the Indian team, following the one led by Tiger Pataudi in the 1960s. Somewhere between Tiger's reign and Ganguly's, India had become a team too easily satisfied, too easily intimidated by the opposition, and perhaps a little too conscious of being nice guys with winning smiles rather than tough competitors who gave no quarter.

Ganguly's team had steel and his own brand of self-confidence. He injected the team with a large dose of self-belief—his waving his shirt was a riposte to Andrew Flintoff, who had done the same in India on the previous tour. Anything you can do, I can with greater fervour and more arrogance, seemed to be Ganguly's mantra. It might have backfired on him if he weren't also successful. But he was, and it didn't.

Ganguly's successors, Rahul Dravid and Anil Kumble, retained the steel and fortified it. They were tough men, but not Ganguly clones. When Ganguly retired, it was clear that the new Ganguly was yet to emerge. 'Such a captain,' I wrote then, 'would be a team-builder, a self-confident manipulator of emotions, a taker of chances, a shirt-waver, metaphorically if not literally. And that pretty much sums up the captain-in-waiting, Mahendra Singh Dhoni. Perhaps

CHAMPIONS!

it is from the Dhoni generation that we will see the full impact of the Ganguly legacy.'

Now that it has come to pass, that Dhoni has taken the team a step further in the World Cup, there cannot be any real surprises. There was an inevitability about the result that robbed it of unexpectedness. Yet neither Dhoni nor his fans will complain. Sporting upsets are fine only so long as it is your team that is doing the upsetting.

The World Cup win is the culmination of a process. One which saw India move up to No. 1 in the world Test rankings, overtaking Australia. When that happened, in December 2009, former skipper Anil Kumble, one of two captains (the other being Ganguly) not in the team then but equally deserving of credit said, 'Almost two years back, we sat down and planned for this day and so you can imagine the feeling among all concerned now that the task has been achieved.' In his usual dignified, understated way, Kumble was pointing out that this was no casual, overnight thing but the result of a well-thought-out set of ideas and their implementation. Mistakes were made, of course, occasionally in team selection, occasionally in tactics, but the overall goal was never lost sight of. Success is never accidental, and to attribute India's success to luck and happy circumstance is unfair to the players and coaches who put so much effort into it.

Under Ganguly, India travelled better, winning matches with consistency outside the subcontinent; under Dravid, the victories in the West Indies and England, achieved by Ajit Wadekar's team in 1971, were duplicated after three decades. Kumble brought to the team a vision for the future and a statesman-like texture to captaincy. By the time Dhoni took over, the ground had been prepared; he is a young man leading a mature team, bringing youth's flamboyance and ability to walk on the edge to the range and ability to calculate risks that experience makes possible.

The Test ranking rubbed off on the one-day attitude. In 2010, India sent a second-string team to Zimbabwe for a tri-series. The aim was not so much to win the tournament, but to give promising youngsters a chance to break into the big league. Suresh Raina, who captained the side, said at the start that it was a wonderful opportunity for India's medium pacers.

As it happened, India did not make it to the final, after losses to both Zimbabwe and Sri Lanka, but crucial lessons were learnt. Only four players from that squad made it to the World Cup—Kohli, R. Ashwin and Yusuf Pathan were the others—and the medium pacers suggested they were not yet ready.

To lose a battle in pursuit of victory in the larger war was an occupational hazard for a team that had its sights firmly fixed on winning the World Cup. In the end, it didn't matter where it began—1983 or 2002 or 2007. What mattered was where it ended. ■

Y And Z And The X-Factor 4

A decade-long apprenticeship pays off

Two men who made their international debut in the same match more than a decade ago played key roles in India's victory. Both Zaheer Khan and Yuvraj Singh announced their arrival in the ICC Knockout tournament in Kenya. Zaheer was a hit straightaway in India's first match against Kenya, with three wickets for 48. Yuvraj didn't have to wait long. His 84 against Australia hinted at the nightmare he would become to bowlers in the shorter form of the game for years to come.

Yuvraj finished as the Player of the Tournament at the World Cup, with a tally of 362 runs and 15 wickets. Before the start, India had no all-rounders; now suddenly they had a world-class one (at least on the subcontinent's wickets).

In a tournament expected to be dominated by spinners, medium pacer Zaheer Khan emerged as the top wicket-taker (sharing the honour with Pakistan's Shahid Afridi who, too, had 21 wickets).

For some years now, Zaheer Khan has been not only the spearhead of the Indian attack but the fountainhead of its fast bowling wisdom. His role before the tournament began was simple: he would set the ball rolling, pick up a wicket or two and then stand aside while the spinners dismissed the opposition on the helpful tracks. Good theory, but it didn't take into account two factors.

One, the helplessness of India's main spinners and two, Zaheer's own combativeness. He may not have the pace of a Shaun Tait or be as quietly intimidating as Dale Steyn, but he has skills neither does; among them, the ability to surprise with a delivery that refuses to give up its secrets till it's too late for the batsman to do anything about it. It was said of Anil Kumble that he was a spinner with the aggressive intent of a fast bowler. Zaheer is the reverse—a fast bowler with the subtlety and variety of a spinner. A master at deceiving the batsman into thinking a ball is arriving faster or slower than he thinks it is.

CHAMPIONS!

The West Indies opener D.S. Smith, Australia's Mike Hussey and Sri Lanka's Chamara Kapugedera will all testify to the efficacy of Zaheer's slower delivery. Each was fooled and dismissed at crucial stages of the innings.

By the end of the tournament, Zaheer, 32, was being seen as the finest bowler of his type in the world. Others might be faster, but he was more dangerous; others might intimidate, he would confuse.

Together, Yuvraj, now 29, and Zaheer discovered that the planets were in the right alignment, the stars had taken their appointed slots and everything was ready for the big moment. Their decade-old apprenticeship at the highest level was about to pay off.

Remarkably, Zaheer didn't fail in a single game of the nine. That he played all of them was surprising in itself, considering the spate of injuries he had suffered in recent years. Also, while the rest of the team was determined to erase the terrible memories of the 2007 campaign which ended before the knockout, Zaheer was still coming to terms with the personal ghosts of the 2003 final. His first over then had ten deliveries and went for 15 runs. It wasn't just the pressures of the final, it was also the pressure to perform after skipper Sourav Ganguly had put Australia in. The fast bowler was keyed beyond adequacy.

India never recovered from Australia's 74 without loss in nine overs. Till eight years later. Till Zaheer Khan had added to his repertoire the ball that ducked back into the right-hander from over the wicket, and more significantly, the one that started off in a hurry and then slowed down to force the batsman into committing early. Eight years later, he was more mature, less excitable, and more determined now that he knew where things could go wrong.

The contrast between 2003 and 2011 was startling. This time Zaheer began with three maidens in a row and the wicket of Upul Tharanga. His last two overs went for 35, but he had done enough in the first eight for India to keep their grip on the game.

The Zaheer motif had been painted in the tied match against England in Bangalore, easily the match of the tournament. England were 280 for two in the 43rd over, chasing India's 338, when Zaheer Khan turned it around with two wickets in two balls, getting the two top scorers. Skipper Andrew Strauss had made 158 and Ian Bell 69. Zaheer first had Bell caught at extra cover and then Strauss leg before to a late swinging yorker. India were back in the game.

This was a pattern that India began to take for granted as the tournament progressed. When they found themselves in trouble, Zaheer Khan came to them. He didn't merely restore sanity with a tight spell, he claimed the crucial wickets.

But it wasn't just Zaheer the bowler who was important to India's plans. There was Zaheer the bowling captain, the man who mentored the other medium pacers, running up to them with advice, sometimes setting the field for them, and at all times inviting them to dip into his vast bag of experience for anything they might find useful. This generosity has been an underplayed aspect of Zaheer's cricket. Senior players, especially bowlers, usually have a standard approach to mentoring youngsters: watch and learn.

Zaheer always went a step or two further. Learn, and if you don't get it, keep asking questions. The faster man, Sreesanth, is perhaps more naturally gifted, but his ideal is Zaheer and he wants to be like his hero. Zaheer, who has had to learn his craft on his own (a stint in the English county helped,

as he says, because he could experiment, something he didn't have the luxury of doing in India), is happy to share his special knowledge with colleagues.

Zaheer Khan is the cricketer's cricketer, and such men tend to be overlooked when it is time to hand out the kudos. His art is not immediately apparent, for its speciality is in concealing art. His craft has been honed over the years by adding a skill here, eliminating a weakness there, and readjusting something else. Bowling is a difficult craft. Everything is down to a matter of angles and inches. A couple of inches and the ball will take the edge of the bat, another inch and it will miss it altogether. Zaheer, who had to choose between a career in engineering and cricket, is the game's engineer, having worked out the angles and inches that matter.

Not for him the flamboyance of a Yuvraj Singh or the all-rounder's sense of entitlement. Commitment came naturally to the left-arm seamer, not so easily to the left-arm spinner. But when it happened, it did simultaneously, and the Indian team benefited.

Being Yuvraj

The resurrection of Yuvraj has been one of the inspiring stories of the World Cup. Down, and nearly out six months ago, he transformed into a champion in a champion side. It must have been difficult, and it is possible he learnt as much from Tendulkar, who inspired him, as from the younger players who held up a mirror to his own flashy ways.

Whenever there is a breach in the wall of platitudes around a cricketer, it is time to sit up and take notice. Modern players say the expected things in the expected manner so everybody is happy. Yet, occasionally, a desire to make sense triumphs, as it did with Yuvraj in an interview he gave in 2010, his annus horribilis, when nothing went right for him and he lost his place in the Indian team.

It is worth quoting the interview he gave to the website cricinfo at some length. 'I see a lot of youngsters like Virat Kohli and Rohit Sharma, who are very talented and flamboyant. As a senior I tell them not to make the same mistakes I made, and try to guide them to a better tomorrow. When I began playing, you could say the game was changing, the distractions were beginning. Now the distractions are too much and my advice to the younger guys is mostly not to be distracted by what is happening outside and to concentrate on the game.

CHAMPIONS!

'They don't listen, especially Rohit and Virat. [Suresh] Raina still listens a little bit, but Rohit and Virat always argue with me. I don't blame the youngsters for not listening, because a lot of times Sachin or Sourav or Kumble said something to me and I said, "What do they know?" As a senior, I think it's our duty to help the junior guys. Hopefully they'll listen, if not to me, to other players.'

Yuvraj went on to speak about greed and an ever-expanding list of must-haves from houses to cars and partying at the cost of missing practice, and the need to have a balance.

'I fear for the youngsters. If there were fifty per cent distractions in cricket 10 years ago, today they are at one hundred per cent. Any youngster can fall out anywhere. Especially since the IPL, a lot of youngsters, particularly in first-class cricket, focus on the IPL, which is a very bad thing. The players feel that they are not good enough in international cricket and they can survive in the IPL.'

That it took a Yuvraj Singh to give breath to the unspoken was amazing. Many hoped he would follow his own advice. For long he had been considered the bad boy of Indian cricket, distracted by the attractions around it and liable to sink his enormous gifts in a vat of such attractions.

Yuvraj's talent was never in doubt but there were question marks over his commitment, his fitness, his motivation. Before the World Cup began, jokes about his excess weight and reduced mobility (to put these things politely) were the staple of SMS jokes. More depressingly, this star, who already had a place in an all-time Indian ODI XI, had played just five of India's 32 matches as the team was preparing to claim the World Cup. Injuries included a fracture of the hand, a wrist injury and a neck strain. Confidence was low. Yuvraj hadn't scored a century in nearly two years, and kept his spirits up by telling himself over and over again, 'Tough people outlast tough times.'

The World Cup transformation was therefore all the more stunning. In the final, Yuvraj's fielding in the 30-yard circle was inspirational, and appropriately enough, he was there at the end to see the team through. Afterwards he thanked his spiritual guru Baba Ajit Singh for his transformation and success. But it was not a smooth ride. Dehydration during his century against the West Indies forced him to take some time off to throw up on the field. That was not all. 'He has been vomiting a lot,' his skipper Dhoni told the media later. 'Yes, the anxiety can be really heavy,' Yuvraj confessed.

Yuvraj combined the fearlessness of youth with the maturity that comes with experience to live the role that was written for him. That of being the finisher, the one who sees the team through. He remained unbeaten in four of his eight innings, and India lost the only match—against South Africa—where he failed, not contributing with either bat or ball. He made 12 and went wicketless.

Against the West Indies, India were 51 for two and in dire need of a batsman to shore up the middle order when Yuvraj provided that service. In a partnership worth 122 with Kohli, he first steadied the ship and then watched helplessly as India managed to lose seven wickets for 50. Against Australia, with India needing 72 from 67 balls, he struck fast bowler Shaun Tait arrogantly—and joyously—over point to open the floodgates. His unbeaten 57 and a magical 74-run partnership with Raina suggested that India could go all the way.

But it was Yuvraj's bowling that came as a surprise. From an occasional left-arm spinner who might be pressed into action to share ten overs with another part-timer, he quickly emerged as a frontline bowler, picking the right length to bowl on the Indian tracks. His success pushed into the background the relative failure of the man who was expected to spearhead the spin bowling, Harbhajan Singh, who spent much of the World Cup caught between the two stools of run-denying and wicket-taking, accomplishing neither to his satisfaction.

CHAMPIONS!

Y AND Z AND THE X-FACTOR

Yuvraj's five for 31 against Ireland brought down to earth the team which had just beaten England. On a dry track which promised spinners some help, it was only Yuvraj who seemed to hold the key to its secrets. Not a great turner of the ball, he varied both speed and length, giving the impression of great honesty while turning out to be deceptive in his methods. When he caught and bowled Kevin O'Brien, the man who had destroyed England, only the mopping-up operations remained.

Interestingly, while Yuvraj reconnected with his free-stroking past, with what he was before injury and attitude became handicaps, Zaheer took advantage of what he had become, a scholar in the art of taking wickets on difficult tracks. It was a combination that meshed well. ∎

The Quiet Motivator 5

Coach Gary Kirsten combined the best of two worlds

When Gary Kirsten was carried on the shoulders of his players after India's win, the look of surprise on his face was genuine. Unlike coaches who are magnanimous in defeat, willingly sharing the blame with the players while lapping up the kudos solo in victory, he belongs to the old school. One which believes that coaches should neither be seen nor heard. Kirsten, who quickly learnt the ways of Indian cricket, was happy to be the man in the background.

It helped that he had played with some of the seniors and earned their respect as a tough, hard-working batsman for whom nothing came easily, but who made everything count.

Kirsten made his international debut four years after Tendulkar. As a batsman he was at the other end of the spectrum from the Indian, studied where Tendulkar was natural, reined in by limitations where Tendulkar was a free spirit, a percentage player where Tendulkar was a risk-taker.

Regardless of who captained India, it was always important for the national coach to hit it off with Tendulkar. It was not a feat Greg Chappell managed, especially around the time of the previous World Cup. Tendulkar's public support of Kirsten long before this year's edition was critical. He gave the coach the credit for taking India to the No.1 spot in the Test rankings. At an awards function, he said: 'Gary has been instrumental in making our batters play plenty of deliveries in the practice session. During net practice, he himself bowls thousands and thousands of balls.'

After the triumph in Mumbai, Kirsten said, 'It has been a great privilege to coach the Indian team. It has been an honour to be alongside Sachin Tendulkar. He is the greatest sporting role model I have ever met. The passion for the game he has is unparalleled.'

When Kirsten was packing his bags to return home after his successful stint, Tendulkar said,

CHAMPIONS!

'Personally, I would say Gary should continue but he has family commitments. We will miss him a lot. It's been a pleasure to work with him. He has probably worked harder than anyone else.'

Coaching a team of outstanding talents is never easy unless there is a willing suspension of ego. Kirsten is a private man, lacking the natural PR ability of one predecessor, John Wright, or the reverse of that gift that made another, Chappell, stand out. He had more depth than the former and was more accessible than the latter, which in a national team oozing with self-confidence was exactly the combination that was needed in a coach.

It is never easy being the coach of the Indian side. Both players and officials test you to see just how far they can push you and get away. Fans are demanding and the media spotlight never leaves you. If you are a mix of Machiavelli, Mother Teresa, Nelson Mandela and Muhammad Ali it might help, but even then, success is not guaranteed.

In *Indian Summers* (Penguin Books India; 2006), his account of coaching India, Wright has written about selection meetings: 'It was easy to tell when selectors had come to a meeting with an agenda, i.e., to try their damnedest to get one or two players from their zones into the team. If their boys weren't picked, they tended to cross their arms, clam up and take no further part in the meeting.'

More tellingly, he wrote about how he was met with a limousine at the airport when the Indian team won, and was forced to take a taxi on his own when they lost. The lonely figure at an airport trying to hail a taxi has been the symbol of the Indian cricket coach since—the rich possibilities always came with statutory warnings.

THE QUIET MOTIVATOR

Kirsten could not have been unaware of this. First there was the self-coaching: how to handle India and Indians without the cultural snafus that reduced a fine coach like Chappell into a defensive, self-justifying object of derision. The actual cricket was the least of the problems, since these were professional players who knew what they were doing. Perhaps 'coach' is a misnomer. 'Mentor' would be more appropriate.

Kirsten brought to his job an instantly recognized honesty and a realistic appraisal of his place in the scheme of things. He treated the players like adults, knowing all the while just how childish they could sometimes be. He won their respect and gratitude by refusing to preach from Olympian heights and by leaving his ego back home in Cape Town. He has been characterized as being 'egoless', which is unique among the raging egos that all successful sporting teams are built around. Above all, he empowered the players, gently getting them to arrive at their own conclusions, nudging them in the direction of solutions they would discover themselves and refusing to talk down to them.

'He gave the players a lot of personal responsibilities,' said Rahul Dravid, former captain, whose work ethic closely resembles that of Kirsten's. 'Within certain boundaries, the onus was on the players to be responsible for their performances and preparations.'

This is a revolutionary concept in India where, right from school, promising cricketers are squeezed into a system of do's and don'ts that they are discouraged from questioning till they reach a stage when they cannot think without the aid of a coach.

CHAMPIONS!

It helped that Kirsten had played over a hundred Tests and scored over 14,000 international runs in both forms of the game. His 275 against England after following on in Kingsmead in the 1999-2000 series remains the second-longest Test innings after Hanif Mohammed's 999-minute 337 for Pakistan against the West Indies in 1957-58. It took 14 and a half hours. Self-denial came easily to Kirsten; if there was a job to be done, he brought to it oodles of common sense and remarkable focus, two qualities the Indian team imbibed from him.

It was what Kirsten was not, however, that endeared him to the team. He was not a martinet, imposing his will on a bunch of wonderfully gifted players. He recognized that players like Tendulkar and Dhoni are self-regulating mechanisms that don't need constant attention. He was not a father figure, remote and sanctified by age and experience. He was there for the players any time they needed him, but as a friend, not as a head priest and headmaster rolled into one.

He was not a bore on technique, harping on the one and only way in which things ought to be done. Before a series against Sri Lanka, he advised the players not to watch videos of Ajantha Mendis, suggesting that they should play him without the baggage of excessive scrutiny. No paralysis by analysis for him or, by extension, for the team.

You can be a great coach without being a good human being, but players, certainly Indian players, prefer a good human being who is not on an ego trip. In return, they are willing to play out of their skins. It was a lesson Wright learnt in time, and Kirsten picked up very early. In between, Chappell refused to understand that, and despite putting in place many of the systems—player rotation, changing of batting orders, fielding practises—that bore fruit at the World Cup, his reign was ultimately a failure after a promising start.

Tendulkar has credited Kirsten with aiding his second coming as a great batsman, for helping him deal with short-pitched bowling and for the ritual throw-downs before every game that both relax and focus the batsman.

Sunil Gavaskar was impressed by the fact that not once in his tenure did Kirsten wear the India cap; it is a small thing, but India have suffered a coach in the past who wanted to go out and toss in place of the captain.

CHAMPIONS!

The foreign hand

The foreign coach is not a foreign concept in Indian cricket. Before their first Test tour in 1932, the Indian players were put through their paces by the Australian Frank Tarrant, an all-rounder for Victoria and Middlesex who served as the cricket aide to the Maharajas of Cooch Behar and Patiala. 'A canny advisor and an astute lobbyist with impeccable connections, Tarrant helped lay the foundations of Indian cricket,' wrote Mike Coward in *Cricket Beyond the Bazaar* (Allen & Unwin; 1990), his book on the Indo-Aussie relationship. Tarrant also umpired the first Test on Indian soil, in Bombay in 1933-34.

Kirsten was merely the latest—and the most successful—in the list of foreign coaches. He laid great stress on building relationships and earning the trust of the players. He spent time trying to understand the Indian way, and learnt that compromise and that wonderfully untranslateable English word in this context, 'adjustment', was what it was all about.

'Adjustment' involves a bit of mutual back-scratching, the ability to ignore irritants so long as they don't interfere too much with the main vision, the apparent willingness (not to be confused with genuine willingness) to appear 'reasonable' while being focussed on the progress of the team. Kirsten might have lacked subtlety as a batsman, but his man-management skills were subtle and effective. Remarkably, he left India without having made a single enemy. Possibly a greater achievement than coaching the team to the World Cup!

Like an Indian wedding which is not just between the bride and the groom but involves two families, coaching India is not just about the cricket. The more difficult task is the handling of the officials, and here Kirsten's throw-downs were impeccable.

It didn't matter if he didn't get credit for a particular selection or a specific decision, he ensured that in the end the team had the right players in the right slots. He never went public with his criticism except once, when he complained that at 43 he was still fitter than some of the Indian players.

His philosophy was summarized in an interview he gave cricinfo after the final: 'People need to trust that if they made errors the environment would not come hard at them. They would know we believed in each individual and we supported them. It was not to make people comfortable; it was to give people structure. It was to tell people they were moving towards something other than their individual glory.'

He kept count of the unforced errors the team made on the field and celebrated when it dropped from 12 runs to five. His mental training expert Paddy Upton persuaded the Arctic explorer Mike Horn to give inspirational talks to the team. With Upton, Kirsten formed a partnership that took in both the physical and the psychological aspects of training. Not bad for someone who had no experience in the job before he flew out to India.

There was then, what Kirsten called a 'spread of contributions' that led to victory. While the focus remained on one or two batsmen, it was the success of players like Gambhir, Raina and Kohli that made the difference. Gambhir has spoken of sessions with the coach where he was told he was as good as anybody and an integral part of the team. A crucial 97 in the final was his response.

The Indians are impulse players, realized Kirsten, while the Australians and South Africans tend to plan more. In the coach's evocative words, the 'Indians are in the moment, whereas we are planners.' Kirsten's formula was to combine the best of both worlds.

Had he not been successful, Kirsten would have been remembered as the man who advised the Indian players to have sex to boost on-field performance. He denied it later; it was part of a paper that Upton was circulating. But there was an attractiveness to the idea and a rich vein of humour that was mined the world over. The English off-spinner Graeme Swann congratulated the Indian coach for such forward thinking and hoped other coaches would follow suit.

But in a system that judges only on results, even that would not have mattered. It would not have mattered even if Kirsten recommended mud packs or graffiti-writing as stepping stones to a successful career in cricket. For his record—63 victories in 102 one-day internationals, against 32 losses—suggested a super coach who had all the answers.

The captain-coach relationship is crucial in a team. Ganguly-Wright was excellent, Dravid-Chappell worked well, but it is the Dhoni-Kirsten one that has been the most effective and the least controversial. Captain Cool and Coach Calm had the maths right. ■

A Tournament Of Two Halves

6

How India went from favourites to no-hopers and suddenly looked like champions

Life must be lived forward, but can only be understood backwards. What the Danish philosopher Soren Kierkegaard said in another context applies equally to cricket, and in particular to the World Cup. After the final, it was possible to join the dots, see patterns and speak of inevitability. But joining the dots as they emerged in the league phase would have led to a different picture altogether. It kept the fans on tenterhooks.

As India beat Bangladesh and then tied with England, one thing became depressingly clear. Zaheer Khan apart, they had no bowling worth the name. They allowed Bangladesh to score 283 after Sehwag and Kohli had made centuries in India's 370. Sehwag began the tournament with a boundary, and continued to strike the first ball he received to the fence in four matches thereafter.

Champion teams have the ability to raise their game against tougher opposition. In India's case, a worrying trend began to assert itself early—the tendency to lower the level of their game against lesser opposition. They made heavy weather of scoring just over 200 runs against Ireland in Bangalore. Against the Netherlands, the approach was lackadaisical, even lethargic. At the halfway stage, India, the pre-tournament favourites, assumed the look of a tired team going through the motions.

Things changed dramatically in the knockout. Suddenly there was a spring in the step, the fielding improved beyond recognition and Dhoni began to look and sound like the captain of a champion side now merely filling in the details till the day he would lift the trophy.

This was the same Dhoni who had been saying without any trace of embarrassment that he saw no hope for the fielding of his side, which 'will remain below par'. That meant batsmen needed to score an additional 30 runs per innings to make up. Add to that the lack of firepower in the bowling, which called for another 40 runs, just to be on the safe side. So if the par score at a particular venue was 280 or so, India would have to score at least 350. This, as the skipper himself admitted after the England game, 'is not something we can do every time'.

CHAMPIONS!

Just before the knockout, things were in a state of confusion. Harbhajan Singh, the side's leading spinner, was undecided whether he was a wicket-taker or a run-denier (although the best way to deny runs is to take wickets). Batsmen either played him easily or left him alone as he speared the ball in at them.

It was a phase, too, when the reliance on Tendulkar was overwhelming. First, he was expected to get the team off to a quick start in the company of Sehwag. Then he was expected to calm down and guide the middle order. Finally, he was to ensure that he batted till the 50th over. And occasionally, he was required to turn his arm over when the medium pacers gave the captain grief. The batsman probably bowled the ball of the tournament, spinning one across the face of the bat of a startled

A TOURNAMENT OF TWO HALVES

Michael Clarke. Shane Warne would have been proud of that one.

Against South Africa, at 267 for one, India were fantasizing about a total in excess of 400. Then Tendulkar got out (reminding us that he is human after all), and eight others were so upset they too returned in quick succession to keep the Master company in the pavilion. Nine wickets for 29 runs was the best the team expected to be world champions was able to achieve.

'You don't play for the crowd,' said Dhoni of this harakiri, 'you play for the country.' The suggestion that the batsmen were playing to the gallery is not one that Indian captains make readily, however true it might be.

Batting was meant to be India's strength, but not on the evidence at Nagpur that day on a wicket which held no terrors. Perhaps that was the problem. The Indians believed sheer momentum would carry them through.

So far ahead were the batsmen on the run rate (upwards of seven an over) that a typically Indian attitude was dismissed as a minor glitch at the time. But it was an attitude that had cost them matches

in the past. The habit of slowing down as individual milestones approached. It happened with Tendulkar as he was getting to his 99th international century as well as to Gautam Gambhir en route to his half century.

After the West Indies match, it became clearer than before: India were not the favourites. They struggled against a side which did not play either their best batsman (Chris Gayle) or their best bowler (Kemar Roach), and had to depend on the old reliable Zaheer Khan to pull them back into the game with a crucial wicket when things seemed to be slipping.

Still wide open

No team had shown any marked superiority at this stage. Australia had lost their first match in the World Cup after 12 years, England had lost to Ireland and Bangladesh but beaten South Africa and the West Indies. South Africa hadn't managed to erase their image as chokers, and neither had Pakistan their air of unpredictability. Sri Lanka alone looked good.

Reading the tea leaves after the India-West Indies game didn't tell us anything new. India suggested they might not be overdependent on Tendulkar after all, but it was difficult to shake off the feeling that they continued to be a one-man team. That man kept changing. Against the West Indies it was Yuvraj, even if

A TOURNAMENT OF TWO HALVES

CHAMPIONS!

A TOURNAMENT OF TWO HALVES

his century lacked the fluidity and ease of some of his other efforts. Yet, after the centurion, the flood. It had happened against England, and South Africa too. India lost seven wickets for 50, which one presumes was an improvement, but the problem remained. That of losing wickets in a heap.

Yuvraj falling just before the forced power play in the 46th over meant that India hadn't worked out their power play problem. There was an arbitrariness in taking it that didn't speak too well for the skipper or his coach.

Another element they hadn't mastered was the Decision Review System (DRS). When Edwards was run out (and not given out by the umpire), there was a half-hearted, half-humorous attempt by Munaf Patel to draw attention to it, but no clear-headed decision-making that would have earned India a wicket.

The DRS continued to bug India through the World Cup, although it came to their rescue twice when Tendulkar was given out in the semifinals against Pakistan. Having already made up their minds that it was unreliable, India then refused to try and understand how it could be used to their advantage.

The DRS was used 182 times in the tournament and the umpire's decision was upheld around 80 per cent of the time. But it was changed 37 times, and that is not insignificant. India burnt their hands against England with the leg before appeal against

55

CHAMPIONS!

Ian Bell going against them, although spectators at the stadium could see on the giant replay screen that the ball would have hit the stumps. Turned out, no one knew of the '2.5 metres' rule which said that if the point of impact was beyond two and a half metres, all bets were off since the system was no longer accurate.

In the end, India called for 18 reviews, and had the decision overturned just four times. 'It's a bit confusing,' Yuvraj told the media, probably speaking for his colleagues, 'I don't understand it much.'

At the halfway stage, you could make a list under the heading 'Why India will not win the World Cup' and another under 'Why India will win', and discover a curious overlap. In the former would be such much-discussed drawbacks as playing at home, medium-pace bowling, spin bowling, middle-order batting, fielding, captaincy, and in the other list would be the advantages of playing at home, spin bowling, middle-order batting and captaincy.

This is not as strange as it sounds. When the quarterfinals began, India converted their handicaps into match-winning advantages. Suddenly the somewhat diffused approach was replaced by greater focus and self-belief.

Two things happened before India took on Australia. One of these, the decision to play Suresh Raina, was hailed without reservation. It not only strengthened the middle order and brought another left-hander into the fray, it elevated the level of fielding beyond recognition.

The Indian team that played in the knockout had more or less the same fielders, but it was not the same fielding. Healthy competition was encouraged between the better fielders, Raina, Kohli and Yuvraj. It pulled in its wake the less inspiring efforts of everybody else. By the time India were in the final, they had swung from being one of the worst fielding sides to one of the best. The transformation was both physical and psychological, although it is difficult to say which came first. Not that it mattered. When the call was for raising the standards, India raised the standards, bowling or fielding.

The second event, not as readily acknowledged, was Pakistan's win over Australia in a group match. India's neighbours showed that it could be done, that Australia were vulnerable. It was probably one of the most significant results of the league phase. Australia had not lost in a World Cup since 1992, nor had skipper Ponting had to receive commiserations in 34 matches in a row.

Despite a good record against Australia in recent years, India knew the World Cup was different. Going by the performances in the league, they would have to play out of their skins to tame an Australian side admittedly in decline.

Amazingly, India seemed to solve their problems before millions of eyes. You could see the team emerge from uncertainty to assurance, from one that had been responsible for fans climbing the walls to one that ensured that they got to the roof and stayed there.

Before the start of the World Cup, tournament director Prof. Ratnakar Shetty had said that the format had been tweaked to give the top teams a chance to qualify for the knockout. In a press conference he had stated that 'the exit of India and Pakistan in 2007 was a disaster for the tournament. Sponsors, broadcasters, tour operators, the West Indies Cricket Board, all lost a lot of money.'

The format was big-team friendly in that India could afford to lose three matches in the league and still make it to the knockout (but other things had to fall into place too). And frankly, no team deserved to be there if they had four losses against their name!

India's resurrection meant that there would be interest in the tournament till the end. The team had been given enough rest days between matches and the schedule was not as harsh as it might have been. There was sufficient recovery time.

The win over Australia also meant that India took on Pakistan with an air of superiority that communicated itself to their rivals.

India won the World Cup after systematically defeating all the previous champions—West Indies, Australia, Pakistan and Sri Lanka. There were no lucky breaks, no elimination of strong teams by others to ease the path, and in fact no easy games handed to them on a platter.

Still, it was a tournament of two halves. ∎

Living Up To Expectations 7

The quarterfinals and semis—cricket and beyond

In 1983 it was the West Indies. Once India had beaten them in two out of three matches (the first time in Berbice and the second in Manchester in the World Cup), it was no longer a fantasy to speak of the World Cup and India in the same breath. Likewise, 28 years later. It was when Australia were beaten in the quarterfinals that a measure of certainty crept into India's campaign. Perhaps, more correctly, some of the uncertainty oozed out.

Having played till then like a diffident Clark Kent, they emerged from the experience like Superman from a telephone booth, ready to change the world.

Matches against Australia and Pakistan carry the kind of baggage that sometimes does not fit neatly in any historical or cultural luggage rack. The Pakistan rivalry has gone on for longer, been analysed more and at least acknowledged if not understood. 'More than cricket' is the cliché, although there is always some objective observer who tries to tell anybody willing to listen that the encounter is 'only a cricket match'.

The Australia baggage is lighter and of more recent vintage. For decades, unlike England, Australia respected India enough to send their best teams here on cricket tours. They cribbed less, were more accepting, and when the cycle had turned enough to bring India close to them in the rankings, went public with their pronouncements about the final frontier and so on.

The last Indian tour of Australia with its 'Monkeygate' or accusations of racism against an Indian player, the threat of an Indian withdrawal and the jingoism inspired by the cricket board's stand have all made Australia the country Indians love to hate. Cricket-wise, of course. There is deeper satisfaction in beating Australia today than there was in beating the old colonial masters England in the past. At no point has it been easy, and that has given an Indo-Aussie match a special texture.

CHAMPIONS!

Australia's batting seemed to have taken the game away in the quarterfinal. Their 260—coincidentally the same score India made in the semifinals—might have been a winning score on another day. By chasing it down India hinted, for the first time in the tournament, that they could go all the way. Gone was the diffidence of the league matches; the responsibility for taking the team across the line was spread more evenly and, above all, there was the fielding. Skipper Ponting reckoned after the match that Australia fell some twenty runs short. That was probably the number of runs India saved on the field with a series of dives and dares.

Unlike his predecessor Allan Border, Ponting never managed to become a favourite of Indian crowds. Part of the reason is that he is seen as the personification of all that is the worst of Australian cricket—a no-nonsense, hard-playing, no-quarter-giving, letter-of-the-law-following player who, in the years when Australia was the best team in the world, rubbed it in rather unsubtly.

This is unfair, and often media-inspired. And it takes away from what he is really the personification of—a great batsman capable of shaking off unproductive phases, and exhibiting the hard, unsentimental, champion-like quality of Australian cricket.

The Motera crowd even got into the 'Hai Hai' chant, a recitation of disapproval once reserved for Ravi Shastri in his playing days. But that was the least of Ponting's worries. As an Ashes-losing Australian captain sorely out of form, and potentially a World Cup-losing one too, the cries for his head had grown more strident.

But this was suddenly a changed Ponting. The uncertainty of the earlier matches had disappeared and so, too, the hesitant footwork, the unsure strokeplay. The feet moved, the bat became an extension of the hand, and with every stroke the confidence grew. When he danced down the track to hit Yuvraj inside-out over extra cover, the years fell away, and the 36-year-old looked like he was at the peak of his powers. With that one shot he reduced all speculation about his ability to a joke.

The spinners on a helpful track were given an object lesson in how great batsmen refuse to be tied down. It was an innings of self-denial rather than self-indulgence, and that was easy to understand. Without Ponting Australia might have struggled to make 150; the ease with which he played merely served to show up the ordinariness in the rest of the batting.

CHAMPIONS!

Apparently Ponting prepared for this match by watching his own innings in the 2003 final when his 140 wrenched the game from India from the start. But that was a different kind of knock, full of sixes and arrogant shots. Now he showed another facet of his greatness. The measured, calculating, professional route to a century.

India began well, but three quick wickets in the middle order negated much of the early work and the half centuries by Tendulkar and Gambhir. From 143 for two it was soon 187 for five after Kohli had slammed a full toss down midwicket's throat, Gambhir ran himself out foolishly and Dhoni cut Brett Lee into the hands of the fielder at point.

LIVING UP TO EXPECTATIONS

So far in the tournament no single Indian player had managed to grab it by the neck and take it home with him, as it were. At various times Sehwag, Tendulkar, Zaheer had shown promise of doing so, but now Yuvraj decided to match promise with performance. India needed 74 from the last 13 overs, but they used only ten. Yuvraj played both conductor and lead player of India's chase, talking often to Raina to keep him relaxed. It was the biggest partnership of the match. One Brett Lee over went for 14, and in the end it was mission accomplished with a lot of flair and much care.

Australia had four bowlers capable of bowling at over 140 kmph, but it was like watching an old movie in slow motion. Whatever offie Jason Krejza's qualities, they did not include consistency of line and length. Michael Clarke was the reverse of the perfect all-rounder, in the team neither for his batting nor his bowling. Given a chance to replace a fast bowler with a spinner when Doug Bollinger returned home, Australia had chosen to fly out batsman David Hussey.

While Australia got their balance wrong, India went in the other direction. Yuvraj's confidence as a free-stroking batsman

LIVING UP TO EXPECTATIONS

who had found success rubbed off on his bowling. He was no longer expected to merely go through the motions with as little damage as possible, but to actually take wickets. He began to flight the ball and even bowl slower, a tactic main spinner Harbhajan Singh continued to be innocent of.

The long-awaited inclusion of Ashwin made a difference in two areas. Not only did the off-spinner bowl well, providing the early breakthroughs after opening the bowling, his fielding saved runs in the deep.

India made those small adjustments that make the big difference. They got the team balance right, bringing in the more inventive Raina for the uni-dimensional Yusuf Pathan. Dhoni was more positive than at any other time in the tournament. He attacked more, especially when Ponting was batting.

India still needed the superb Zaheer Khan to take wickets in his second spell to get back into the game. The burden on this willing worker grew through the tournament, but remarkably he delivered every time.

And so to Pakistan.

Sport and politics

Sport is regularly called upon to stand for something other than itself. Nearly seven decades after World War II, England continue to replay the action with Germany on the football field. Cricket (and in the days when their teams mattered, hockey) is the substitute

CHAMPIONS!

in the case of India and Pakistan, who have fought four wars against each other.

No one says, with the conviction of a Gertrude Stein, that a cricket match is a cricket match is a cricket match. And with good reason. The Mohali semifinal was anointed with a significance beyond its status as a sporting encounter, thanks to the presence of the prime ministers of India and Pakistan.

Asked on a television show about his reaction to the presence of the dignitaries at the match, the former India wicketkeeper Syed Kirmani thought for a moment and said, 'I would like to avoid these political questions. Ask me anything you want about the cricket.'

He was speaking for the players of both teams, who have the kind of relationship that professionals anywhere have with their rivals, but who are sometimes expected to be overly aggressive and jingoistic for commercial purposes. The media demand a macho image and build their advertising budgets based on that!

An encounter like this shows up the strain between the demands of commerce and politics. What is politically correct need not be commercially so, and vice versa.

Over the years, it has become impossible to discuss an India-Pakistan match in purely cricketing terms. Clichés abound. There is talk of temperament. There is the rather silly notion of countries defining their nationhood, manhood and womanhood through the activities of a bunch of often undereducated sportsmen in a game that is so dependent on chance.

It has long seemed to me thoroughly illogical that two sovereign nations should seek validation through victory

LIVING UP TO EXPECTATIONS

on the sports field. When India play Pakistan, everybody—the players, the media, the politicians, the big business, that beast known as the man in the street—everybody assumes the stand he is expected to. Over the years I have probably written variations of this myself. This is the true joy of an India-Pakistan cricket match. It gives all of us an opportunity to slip into our predetermined roles.

In 1996, when Pakistan lost, their national television played mournful tunes. Wasim Akram, who missed the match with injury, received death threats. A cartoon in a newspaper gave a twist to the promise of a 'plot for every player' if Pakistan won, showing freshly dug graves.

In India we felt smug and superior. It lasted till the next match, which Sri Lanka were awarded following crowd agitation. We were brought down to earth quickly. We were genuinely brothers under the skin, unable to take defeat with grace.

'The Indian mood swing, from elation in Bangalore to enraged despair in Kolkata, would be categorized by psychoanalysts as a symptom of paranoid schizophrenia. And the virulent manner in which the erstwhile gods of Pakistani cricket were turned upon by their devotees displayed the same syndrome,' wrote Mike Marqusee in his account of the 1996 World Cup, *War Minus the Shooting* (Mandarin; 1996). He also pointed out that two suicides were reported—one in India and another in Pakistan—as the respective teams bowed out.

Sport carries a heavy burden when it is so pregnant with symbolism that the ordinary is often brushed aside.

67

LIVING UP TO EXPECTATIONS

A strange innings

After a languid, meandering league, the tournament had burst into life. The two longest-serving champions, the West Indies and Australia, who between them had won two-thirds of the World Cups, had been eliminated. And the dream match in the subcontinent (which didn't take place in 1987 or 1996 because the fond hope was that the teams would meet in the final rather than earlier) had come to pass.

Would Tendulkar make his 100th international hundred in Mohali? Not if we can help it, said Afridi, the Pakistan captain.

What a strange little innings that was from Tendulkar! Even his greatest fans probably hoped the landmark wouldn't come here. Not after the DRS rescued him twice, and after four different fielders dropped catches he offered with such metronomic regularity.

The sheer embarrassment finally got to him. Great players tend to believe that the means are as important as the end. In this they differ from the merely professional who believe that the end justifies the means. Tendulkar is both a great player and a very professional one; the two qualities are not always in opposition. But against Pakistan they were.

And yet he nearly made a century while struggling thus, and that was remarkable. A professional, we have been told, is someone who does a job even when he doesn't feel like it, and Tendulkar's ability to carry on said something about the kind of person he is.

As a batsman who likes to show the bowler who is boss and lower the boom on him, Tendulkar loves to play the difficult shots, hit the good balls to the fence, as he did throughout this tournament. But, as a professional, he is willing to grind it out in the larger interest. So he is happy to sometimes play the ordinary shot, the one expected of lesser batsmen, if that is the safer option.

He struggled to read Saeed Ajmal's off-spin, was beaten by the doosra and might have been stumped, but the DRS, which he has done much to keep away from India's matches outside the World Cup, saved him.

CHAMPIONS!

Every time he was dropped off Afridi, he exchanged wry smiles with the Pakistani captain, who seemed to suggest he ought to invest in a lottery ticket on this lucky day of his.

Yet when he drove, especially past cover, or delicately late cut past the wicketkeeper, he was the recognizable Tendulkar, if not quite the man who put Shoaib Akhtar in his place in the 2003 World Cup. That was a coruscating innings, this one blinked with the irregularity of poorly connected Christmas lights.

The Australian leg-spinner Arthur Mailey once said, 'I'd rather spin and see the ball hit for four than bowl a batsman out by a straight one.' Tendulkar might say, in similar vein, 'I'd rather see a perfect cover drive go straight to a fielder than get a boundary off an inner-edge.'

Against Pakistan, he did both, and as sometimes happens, fortune favoured the embarrassed.

After the match, Dhoni confessed that he had misread the wicket, but once again it was medium pace rather than spin which delivered. Ashish Nehra, pilloried after his 16-run final over against South Africa, finished with two for 33, Munaf Patel had two for 40. It was just enough to carve the heart out of the Pakistani chase.

A Call For Magnanimity 8

Navel-gazing and money-making versus responsibilities to the game

South Asia—with three teams in the semifinals of the World Cup—clearly have the power. But are they aware that it comes with responsibility? That this is the nerve centre of cricket has been obvious for nearly two decades now. India is where the money is, and the passion is spread over Bangladesh, Pakistan and Sri Lanka too. The tournament has put the stamp of Asian dominance over an English sport.

The future of cricket will depend on how well the region handles this power. The prognosis is not very encouraging. Match-fixing and its cousin, spot-fixing, have been rampant. Three Pakistani players, Salman Butt, Mohammed Asif and Mohammed Amir, have been banned and face trial in a British court. No country is willing to tour Pakistan after the attack on the Sri Lankan team bus in Lahore. Pakistan play their matches abroad and are entitled to their share of the financial returns. But where does all that money go?

The administrators are a disaster. That fine cricket writer Osman Samiuddin wrote of Ijaz Butt, the chairman of the Pakistan Cricket Board, that 'a more damaging tenure in the PCB's history has not been seen,' adding, 'Because of him, world cricket bodies will not work with Pakistan.' Butt had accused England of somehow being responsible for the spot-fixing. 'Anyone but us' is a common but pathetic theme.

Before the India-Pakistan match in Mohali, Pakistan's interior minister declared that he was monitoring the players closely in case they were about to indulge in a spot of match-fixing. His advice to them: Don't do it.

In Sri Lanka, the sports minister called the country's cricket board 'the third most corrupt institution in the country'. (The other two were education and the police.) Sri Lanka have been getting along with an 'Interim Committee' since 2005, with no sign of elections to the cricket board.

CHAMPIONS!

India are guided by intense self-interest and money-grabbing. Former India captain Tiger Pataudi has said that the ICC might be the voice of cricket, but the Indian board is the 'invoice' of the game. 'It is time we had a proactive, eloquent and constructive BCCI,' he urged. Also one that is transparent and accountable.

The four countries that hosted the World Cup are in the bottom half of Transparency International's Annual Corruption Index. India are 87th, Sri Lanka are 91st, Bangladesh 134th and Pakistan 143rd. Against this background, what are the odds that the millions generated by the game are being put back into the game?

Sri Lanka's Arjuna Ranatunga is clear: 'The money that comes from TV rights deals,' he has said, 'has gone into the pockets of some individuals.'

Will the World Cup success make matters worse, the corruption intolerable, the parochialism go unchecked, the muscle-flexing interminable, or will it inspire a change, a new maturity, a more confident, inclusive world view?

Whose game is it anyway?

Does cricket belong to the international stars, the journeymen players, the officials, the fans who make possible the lifestyles of the rich and famous, or to all of them? The stakeholders are in the millions, yet the power is concentrated in the hands of a few in India whom the international body dare not displease. Players, who bring the thousands into the stadiums, have no say in the development of the game. They are treated like prize cows, moved around from fair to fair, while the organizers make the money. One of the saddest lines to emerge at the World Cup came from Paul Collingwood's daughter, who hoped that England would lose a key match so that she could have her father home earlier.

India have the power to sort out many of the ills of the game. The excessive, often disorganized touring, the illegal betting and spot-fixing, chucking, and many more. But often they have chosen to be part of the problem, rather than finding a solution; technical committees cleared the action of Shoaib Akhtar because it was politically expedient to do so at the time.

A CALL FOR MAGNANIMITY

India have got to where they have by dint of hard work and accidents of history like the arrival at the same time of Sachin Tendulkar and a host of great batsmen and bowlers. The economic liberalization brought in a new confidence and large disposable incomes. Till 1993, India paid their national broadcaster to televise cricket matches. Then the board decided to sell the TV rights, and earned millions of dollars. The government, in its wisdom, quoted an 1885 Act to keep its monopoly, but a century later the country had moved on and government bullying was not well received.

Ever since Jagmohan Dalmiya improved the ICC finances when he became president—from 16 thousand to 16 million pounds—the talk was of spreading cricket to 'new markets'. Ever since, thanks to India's enormous people power, financial power, television and sponsorship power,

The old order changes... Jagmohan Dalmiya arrives for a meeting with Malcolm Gray

CHAMPIONS!

they have been a super-ICC. They have had umpires changed, Test matches cancelled, decisions twisted in their favour; they have threatened and waved money under the noses of people to get their way, and ensured the mix of nationalism and commerce is always kept well stirred to generate greater jingoism and more money.

The ICC, realizing where the power lay, rode piggyback on India's entrepreneurial and manipulative skills. The ICC is not in love with India, and does not follow the country's dictates merely because the time has come. No, it is the money which speaks in the one case and causes a holding of the tongue in the other.

It is notable, too, that the democracy that India fought for in the ICC is conspicuous by its absence both in the Indian board as well as in the treatment of the ICC and other boards by India.

The Supreme Court recently upheld a Kerala High Court decision that cricket officials are public servants and can be tried under the Prevention of Corruption Act, which applies only to public servants. This is good news. Especially when you consider what the income-tax authorities have told us: the BCCI spends just eight per cent of its revenues on the promotion of cricket!

A CALL FOR MAGNANIMITY

CHAMPIONS!

The nature of the beast

The cyclical nature of sporting dominance is obvious to anyone who has followed a team for any length of time. That is what gives teams in decline—like Australia now in cricket—the strength to carry on, secure in the knowledge that their time will come, the right players will emerge, the encouraging results will follow. But there is another cycle that is not always commented on. That is the cycle of administrative dominance.

In the years when England and Australia were the top teams, England ran the game from a backroom at Lord's as if by divine right. This entitlement was reinforced by the political reality of Britannia ruling the waves. They occasionally waived the rules too, but lesser countries could do nothing.

You don't need to have read Mike Marqusee's *Anyone But England* (Aurum Press; 2005) to understand the manner in which England used to treat cricketing countries like India. Long after the non-white colonies gained independence, England continued to behave as if history had stopped with the ascension of Queen Victoria to the throne.

The Imperial Cricket Conference became the International Cricket Council in two steps spread over 34 years, the word 'Imperial' having been dropped in 1965. But it was not until 1993, when England and Australia lost the power of veto, that the ICC started to become a democratic body, a full 84 years after it was established. In that time, two Asian countries, India (1983) and Pakistan (1992), had already won the World Cup.

Now, things are moving Asia-wards at all levels. Before this World Cup began, India had become the No.1 Test-playing country. The president of the ICC is an Indian, Sharad Pawar. The two cycles have finally begun to move together in unison. Dalmiya took over as the president in 1997; it has taken the players this long to ensure that performances on the field match the manoeuvres off it.

However, India's dominance will be meaningless if it is not used constructively for the good of the game, not only in the region but worldwide. Already the game is in some disarray in the Caribbean, with the supply lines beginning to dry up and talented international players like Chris Gayle more interested in personal aggrandizement than in inspiring the national team to victories. He has said often enough that he would rather play in the IPL than represent his country. It is a theme that will grow louder with time.

Indians atop the ICC pile...
Jagmohan Dalmiya and Sharad Pawar

CHAMPIONS!

Business and Bollywood, part of the IPL mix

Increasingly, the temptation to make in some six weeks of the IPL the kind of money that might take a year or three to earn is turning the heads of many players. Javed Miandad thinks the IPL is the main cause of Australia's decline. That might be an extreme view, fuelled by the No-Pakistani attitude of the IPL, but the fact remains that of the three formats of the game, the one that thrives will be the one that India throw their weight behind.

Sensible planning can accommodate all three formats, but 'sensible' and 'planning' are not words that go together well in the Indian context. India are happy to play interminable one-day series against Sri Lanka if it suits them, or make a shambles of the Future Tours Programme of the ICC if that works best.

A CALL FOR MAGNANIMITY

Self-interest and money-making have been the BCCI's dominant themes, but the time has come to shed the baggage of colonialism and stop seeing everything—from players being fined for minor transgressions to umpiring decisions—as insults to the nation. India have played the victim long enough.

It was a ploy that worked well for Dalmiya, both as a populist move at home and for muscle-flexing purposes abroad. But the Indian board has to change its essentially selfish stance and accept its responsibility as a leading player in the world game with responsibilities to the game itself. This is not the time for narrow, provincial games intended to score points off rivals in a clash of egos. India must develop the mindset to think big—and not just financially.

This is not to say that when they ran the game, England were the epitome of virtue and large-heartedness. In fact, it was just the reverse, with the stink of racism, selfishness and exclusivity.

When Sunil Gavaskar said upon first playing at Lord's that it was no big deal, an earlier generation of players and officials had apoplexy. Some years later, when he turned down membership of the MCC because it had treated him badly, many Indians could not believe it. Bishan Bedi took him to task in print for insulting Indian crickethood. The winds of change were blowing gently, but only the sensitive could feel them.

As the 1990s progressed, however, the subtlety went out of the process of change, and it would have needed insensitivity of a high order not to notice that the balance had shifted. Yet it took England an extraordinarily long time to acknowledge this. In his column in the *Times*, the former England captain Michael Atherton finally spelt it out thus: 'India are the big beast of cricket and everyone is frightened of both their bark and bite [...] It was a sweeping change to the balance of power but one that took England, who didn't tour India between 1992 and 2001, a long time to appreciate. [...] Malcolm Speed, the chief executive of the ICC, found himself in a position much occupied by Kofi Annan and the United Nations in recent years: being bullied by a superpower for whom the notions of international law and collective responsibility have long ceased to have any meaning...'

CHAMPIONS!

Indian officials will react by talking about history repeating itself but through different characters. They will insist they are merely following a tradition.

Power play rules

When the West Indies were the leading cricket-playing nation, they had little or no say in its administration. India—and by extension, south-west Asia—have been given a chance to make a difference at a time when they are the top teams in the world, with enormous influence over the way the game is run.

However, if India don't learn to be magnanimous and accommodating, they will lose both their own audience (whom they care little about anyway) and cause a split in the cricketing world, with Australia and England and South Africa deciding, for example, that they can form a circuit without India. Cricket needs variety. Homogeneity is the greatest enemy of competitive sport.

Brinkmanship has been another feature of India's recent approach. True, if India pull out of a World Cup, the tournament would collapse. Yet, in 1996, after what Graham Halbish, former CEO of the Australian Cricket Board called a 'decidedly ugly ICC meeting in London', Australia, England, New Zealand and the West Indies were prepared to break away from the ICC.

In Halbish's book, *Run Out* (Lothian Books; 2003), he gives the details of 'Project Snow', a 'genuine option for Australia and their closest allies to counter a power play by the subcontinent and South Africa'. Was this done to save the game? Here's what Halbish says: 'The contingency plan would allow us to keep satisfying our television networks, sponsors and crowds.' Note the order.

'Project Snow would provide our group with three outcomes we believed were necessary: First, to show South Africa they had chosen the wrong side; second, to steady India and the subcontinent's quest for more influence over all matters cricket; and third, to restore balanced leadership to international cricket,' Halbish writes, blissfully unaware of the irony. Is it any wonder then, that given the chance, India are happily putting the Englands and Australias in their place?

If Project Snow tells us anything, it is that angels and devils are interchangeable in cricket; today's angel is often tomorrow's devil, and both are driven by the same motive. It is not unusual for the one paying the piper to call the tune.

Yet, this is where the South Asian countries can change things. Cricket cannot progress if the mistakes of the past are endlessly repeated by the new power centres. Someone has to break that cycle. The Asian power houses have been given an opportunity to do so. And that is the real significance of their World Cup success, on and off the field.

The question that many may ask at this point is: Should the BCCI be so concerned about world cricket when its brief is Indian cricket? As long as Indian cricket is served, why worry? Countries construct their diplomacy and economic policies on the foundation of self-interest, so why should sport be different?

The answer is simple. As the world champions and the No.1 Test-playing country, with the power and influence that comes with having the richest cricket board in the world, the BCCI must give up their narrow-minded domestic concerns and focus on cricket, the world game. Whatever the compulsions of political entities in the United Nations, sport must follow the beat of a different drum. For that is the reason for its existence—it is artificial and should strive to be idealistic.

Also, what goes around will come around as boards that ruled in the past have discovered. India will not be on top forever, and countries at the top have a responsibility to the game beyond concerns for their own backyard. A parochial attitude is bound to boomerang. ■

An All-time India XI   9

Only those who've played an ODI need apply

It is a temptation few can resist. From the schoolboy fan to Don Bradman, everyone has indulged in the sport's favourite armchair activity, the choosing of an all-time XI. Bradman, in fact, even suggested teams with players whose names begin with the same letter of the alphabet, or a team of only left-handers, and so on.

No one is immune to the charms of the List. The ICC welcomed the World Cup year by inviting visitors to their website to choose an all-time ODI XI. Around 600,000 'selectors' from 97 countries chose the following combination: Sachin Tendulkar, Virender Sehwag, Brian Lara, Viv Richards, Ricky Ponting, Kapil Dev, Adam Gilchrist, Muthiah Muralitharan, Wasim Akram, Glenn McGrath, Allan Donald. 12th Man: Michael Bevan. The joy of having seven destructive batsmen, each one capable of turning a game around on his own, is that you can have four pure bowlers, the best in the business.

Somehow it is easier to choose an all-time Test XI for a country than it is to arrive at a one-day XI. This is partly because the tactical evolution of the one-day international (which is after all a young game, only four decades old) means that each succeeding generation of players is superior to the previous one. New tactics, better equipment, more focussed strategies, greater fitness levels, all contribute to this. Test cricket evolves more slowly, and it is easier to see in a current player a reflection of an earlier one—Rahul Dravid and Vijay Hazare, for example—because the essentials have remained the same.

This is not so in the shorter form. Already India's first one-day superstar, Krishnamachari Srikkanth, has faded away as a batsman, replaced in the public mind with the more destructive (while being more orthodox) Sehwag.

When India won the World Cup for the first time in 1983, Srikkanth's top score of 38 came in 66 deliveries. It was described as a 'swashbuckling' innings. En route to his superb century against England in the 2011 World Cup, Tendulkar got to his 50 in the same number of deliveries. This was seen as a 'plodding' innings. That's how much the game has changed.

So how do we pick an all-time Indian ODI XI? Although it is tempting to throw the net wide and include all the players who have played for India, only those who have actually played one-day internationals are eligible. Without that rule, we would be going back to C.K. Nayudu, India's first Test captain, Mohammed Nissar and Amar Singh, the fast bowlers who opened in that Test, and the likes of Lala Amarnath, the first Test centurion, Vinoo Mankad, the great all-rounder, and so on.

While all of them were undoubtedly outstanding performers and would have challenged many of the modern heroes, we must draw a line somewhere. India played their first one-day match on 13 July 1974, and our pool contains only those who have represented the country in the shorter game since that date.

The other rule, an obvious one, is that all the players available are at peak form. The eleven should contain: 2 opening batsmen, at least one of whom is a left-hander, 3 middle-order batsmen, at least one of whom bowls, 2 all-rounders, 1 wicketkeeper who can bat, 3 bowlers, with at least one top-class spinner. That is the combination that makes for balance.

Here goes, then.

Sachin Tendulkar: Highest score, most runs, highest number of centuries, most fifties, more matches than anyone else, six World Cups, the only double century in the format, and now, finally a World Cup title. It was only after Tendulkar's debut that India won more matches than they lost; earlier, they hadn't even managed to score 300 in an innings. For a batsman who is the epitome of technical correctness, Tendulkar is also an innovator whose upper cut, the flat-bat pull between the bowler and mid-on and the mischievous paddle sweep have enriched the one-day game. Yet, he has shown repeatedly that big scores can be made in the short game by following the tenets of orthodoxy. He was 37 when he made the game's first double century, an innings straight out of the coaching manual. In a career already 22 years old, he has retained his passion for the game.

AN ALL-TIME INDIA XI

Sourav Ganguly: Matched only by god in his off-side play (in the memorable words of his colleague Rahul Dravid), Ganguly opening with Tendulkar has been one of the great sights of Indian cricket. They have put on more than 5000 runs at nearly 50 per innings, with 16 century partnerships. The left-right combination is guaranteed to irritate the opposition bowlers, especially at the start of the innings with its fielding restrictions. Bowlers have to constantly readjust their line as well as their length, and both Tendulkar and Ganguly are capable of pouncing on the slightest mistake to score runs. In a variety of styles from leg-spin to off-spin and something in between, Sachin has claimed 154 wickets; Ganguly has 100 wickets with his medium pacers. That makes it nearly 30,000 runs and 250 wickets between them. How can you resist that?

Rahul Dravid: One of only five batsmen to score over ten thousand runs in both forms of the game, Dravid can be the old-fashioned anchor or the new-fangled pinch-hitter. But his role here would be to act as the pillar around which the innings is built. With 196 catches, he brings to the team the safest pair of hands in Indian cricket. At slip, his anticipation gives him that split second's advantage that ensures that he doesn't tear either his muscles or his clothes. Dravid's ability to adapt is his greatest gift. He began as a defensive player who was in danger of becoming a prisoner to his technique. But he blossomed after the initial uncertainty into a world-class one-day player who found gaps on both sides of the wicket with ease, and later played the lofted drive into the crowd with stunning casualness. He was the top scorer in the 1999 World Cup with two centuries and a strike rate of 86.

Virender Sehwag: A strike rate of 104 after 236 matches and the ability to thoroughly demoralize the bowling places Sehwag in a special category. When Lasith Malinga bowled him a maiden over in an IPL match, Sehwag said it was the first maiden over he had played in ten years! 'Don't create new strokes when you can get runs easily playing the ones that already exist,' Tendulkar once advised him. Sehwag does both, create the new as well as improve upon the old, and the only one to complain is the bowler. His 175 against Bangladesh in the inaugural match of the 2011 World Cup threatened to spill over into a double century, and for years he was seen as the man most likely to break that barrier. There is a serenity in his approach to the game that is almost Buddha-like; he has the remarkable ability to forget a bad innings or a poor patch. It is impossible to tell watching him in action if he is batting on 150 or has just walked in. Sehwag likes to open in the one-day game, but in this team he will have to play in the middle order to give India a chance for a left-right combination at the top.

1 *Sachin Tendulkar* 2 *Sourav Ganguly* 3 *Rahul Dravid* 4 *Virender Sehwag* 5 *Mohammad Azharuddin* 6 *Yuvraj Singh*
7 *Mahendra Singh Dhoni* 8 *Kapil Dev* 9 *Javagal Srinath* 10 *Anil Kumble* 11 *Zaheer Khan* 12 *Robin Singh*

CHAMPIONS!

Mohammad Azharuddin: As a one-day cricketer, Azharuddin held the Indian batting records before the Tendulkar generation took over. One had to decide whether his involvement with the seedier side of the game in the days when match-fixing threatened to destroy the sport entitled him to a berth here. One of the conditions, we said earlier, was that all players would be in peak form. That means both physical and moral! Azharuddin, probably the best all-round fielder in an Indian team, would make the team on that ability alone, even if he hadn't scored 9378 runs in 334 matches. With Yuvraj and Kapil Dev, Azhar would form a fine fielding triumvirate. Azhar seemed to lack bones, so supple was his body and so fluid his movements. He could whip the ball from outside the off-stump and send it whistling past midwicket. He could move to leg and play the spinner inside out past cover. He was one of India's most pleasing batsmen, whose fatal flaw was not outside the off-stump but inside his head.

Yuvraj Singh: The Player of the Tournament in World Cup 2011 reconnected with his destiny as the finisher of matches for India, a role he had lost sight of for a while. With his ability to lay back and cut fiercely or drive powerfully on the off-side, Yuvraj is the ideal No. 5. Especially since he can guide the bottom half of the batting, much like his skipper M.S. Dhoni, who follows him here. Anyone who hits six sixes in an over in an international match—as Yuvraj did in the T20 World championship four years ago—has to be special. He is slightly ahead of Sehwag in the race to be India's next 10,000-run man, but there is, too, his left-arm spin whose efficacy he rediscovered at the World Cup and which has fetched him 109 wickets so far. An early debut means that after a decade in international cricket, Yuvraj is not yet 30, but has already earned the right to be in an all-time list.

M. S. Dhoni (Captain): First there was the Prudential World Cup, then the Reliance World Cup, and now there is Dhoni's World Cup. In a team with seven India captains, he is the natural choice to lead. There were criticisms in the early phase of the World Cup, but by the end of it Dhoni was hailed as the finest contemporary captain and also the best to have led India. He brings to the job an instinct for the right move and the ability to nurture players, guiding them into form or encouraging them when they are down. As a batsman, a strike rate of 88 is probably a tribute to the manner in which he has curbed his natural attacking game so it dovetails with team interests. Man of the Match in the final for his unbeaten 91, he earned praise for letting his mates wallow in the glory and the public adulation. As batsman, there is nothing Dhoni cannot do; he can defend stoutly if the situation calls for seeing a difficult bowler off or attack joyously if that is the need of the hour. In a few years he might develop into India's finest all-round one-day batsman, and give Tendulkar a run for his money.

AN ALL-TIME INDIA XI

Kapil Dev: The easiest choice for the all-rounder's slot. It was Kapil Dev and his merry band in 1983 who changed a nation's perception of the shorter game. By winning the World Cup he gained it acceptance. As an all-rounder he was one of the best to have pulled on a pair of coloured trousers anywhere. For years, in India, fast bowlers were fast bowlers and batsmen were batsmen—the two seldom came together consistently, although old-timers might bring up the names of Amar Singh and Dattu Phadkar. Kapil went against the Indian stereotype of wristy strokeplayer or mystery spinner, as capable of slogging a fast bowler for six as hitting a batsman on the helmet with a bouncer. For long he was India's most successful one-day captain, having won 56 per cent of the matches he played. At his peak Kapil was a sight to behold. When he played the pull, swivelling with his front leg in the air, it was dubbed the 'Nataraja' shot, uniquely Indian and compressing an age-old posture of Indian dance and sport in one instant.

Javagal Srinath: Only Anil Kumble has taken more than Srinath's 315 wickets, but the fast bowler's strike rate is superior to the spinner's. After enjoying the thrills of pace in the early part of his career, when he was heralded as the fastest bowler to have played for India, Srinath switched to the delights of maturity and experience, discovering the efficacy of the slower ball and the leg-cutter as wicket-taking deliveries. This variety sustained him through the years and he developed into the father figure of India's pacemen as Zaheer Khan, among others, made his international debut. In our team he would be effective both as Kapil Dev's opening partner as well as the first-change bowler who can keep the pressure on by taking wickets.

Zaheer Khan: The modern medium pacer, with the full arsenal of deliveries, including the one that swung the wrong way at his disposal, Zaheer was one of the heroes of the World Cup. His ability to come back and threaten in the second spell set up many Indian victories, especially when the game seemed to be slipping from them. His strike rate of 35 is the best in this side. He has been India's unofficial bowling coach for some years now, and the man younger bowlers turn to for advice and encouragement. Zaheer's weapon has never been pace; it has been deception. After the World Cup he was called the best 130 kmph medium pacer in the world, but he is among the best, whatever the speed.

Anil Kumble: India's most successful bowler in both forms of the game, Kumble didn't need any help from the wicket to be effective. He was quicker than the average spinner, and had all the variations within a small spectrum. He was not a big turner of the ball, nor did he flight it too

CHAMPIONS!

much. He did just enough to beat the middle of the bat and take the edge—a matter of inches, really. Kumble won more matches for India than any other bowler or combination of bowlers, and India's rise as a power fit to rank as No. 1 in the Test world was as much due to him as to the line-up of fabulous batsmen. Batsmen who initially figured that the best way to play him was like a fast off-spinner quickly discovered his deliveries could cleave the air and land at their feet unbidden, to be followed by the inevitable leg before appeal. Kumble had the temperament of a fast bowler, which is what he started out as, and was a tough competitor who once dismissed Brian Lara in a Test match after having his jaw broken and wired. He finished with just under a thousand international wickets.

Robin Singh: 12th Man. An outstanding all-round fielder, Robin was capable of bowling medium pace that occasionally surprised. But it was his batting lower down the order (although his century was made at number three) that drew attention to his skill as someone who always had the big picture in mind.

SCORECARDS

19 February—2 April 2011

Bangladesh v India
19 February
Shere Bangla National Stadium, Mirpur
Toss Bangladesh chose to field
Umpires SJ Davis (Australia) and HDPK Dharmasena (Sri Lanka)

India innings		R	M	B	4s	6s	SR
V Sehwag	b Shakib Al Hasan	175	198	140	14	5	125.00
SR Tendulkar	run out (Shakib Al Hasan/†Mushfiqur Rahim)	28	46	29	4	0	96.55
G Gambhir	b Mahmudullah	39	49	39	3	0	100.00
V Kohli	not out	100	113	83	8	2	120.48
YK Pathan	c †Mushfiqur Rahim b Shafiul Islam	8	10	10	0	0	80.00
Extras	(b 1, lb 2, w 16, nb 1)	20					
Total	**(4 wickets; 50 overs)**	**370**	(7.40 runs per over)				

Did not bat Yuvraj Singh, MS Dhoni*†, Harbhajan Singh, Z Khan, S Sreesanth, MM Patel
Fall of wickets 1-69 (Tendulkar, 10.5 ov), 2-152 (Gambhir, 23.2 ov), 3-355 (Sehwag, 47.3 ov), 4-370 (Pathan, 49.6 ov)

Bowling	O	M	R	W	Econ	
Shafiul Islam	7	0	69	1	9.85	(1nb, 2w)
Rubel Hossain	10	0	60	0	6.00	(5w)
Abdur Razzak	9	0	74	0	8.22	(1w)
Shakib Al Hasan	10	0	61	1	6.10	(3w)
Naeem Islam	7	0	54	0	7.71	
Mahmudullah	7	0	49	1	7.00	(3w)

Bangladesh innings		R	M	B	4s	6s	SR
Tamim Iqbal	c Yuvraj Singh b Patel	70	136	86	3	1	81.39
Imrul Kayes	b Patel	34	33	29	7	0	117.24
Junaid Siddique	st †Dhoni b Harbhajan Singh	37	66	52	1	1	71.15
Shakib Al Hasan*	c Harbhajan Singh b Pathan	55	65	50	5	0	110.00
Mushfiqur Rahim†	c sub (SK Raina) b Khan	25	39	30	2	0	83.33
Raqibul Hasan	not out	28	44	28	0	1	100.00
Mahmudullah	b Patel	6	6	6	0	0	100.00
Naeem Islam	lbw b Patel	2	8	8	0	0	25.00
Abdur Razzak	lbw b Khan	1	6	5	0	0	20.00
Shafiul Islam	run out (Harbhajan Singh)	0	1	1	0	0	0.00
Rubel Hossain	not out	1	4	6	0	0	16.66
Extras	(lb 10, w 13, nb 1)	24					
Total	**(9 wickets; 50 overs)**	**283**	(5.66 runs per over)				

Fall of wickets 1-56 (Imrul Kayes, 6.5 ov), 2-129 (Junaid Siddique, 23.1 ov), 3-188 (Tamim Iqbal, 32.1 ov), 4-234 (Shakib Al Hasan, 39.4 ov), 5-248 (Mushfiqur Rahim, 42.3 ov), 6-261 (Mahmudullah, 44.3 ov), 7-275 (Naeem Islam, 46.3 ov), 8-279 (Abdur Razzak, 47.6 ov), 9-280 (Shafiul Islam, 48.3 ov)

Bowling	O	M	R	W	Econ	
S Sreesanth	5	0	53	0	10.60	(1nb, 1w)
Z Khan	10	0	40	2	4.00	(4w)
MM Patel	10	0	48	4	4.80	
Harbhajan Singh	10	0	41	1	4.10	(1w)
YK Pathan	8	0	49	1	6.12	(2w)
Yuvraj Singh	7	0	42	0	6.00	(1w)

India won by 87 runs
Man of the match V Sehwag (India)

Kenya vs. New Zealand

20 February
MA Chidambaram Stadium, Chepauk, Chennai
Toss Kenya chose to bat
Umpires M Erasmus (South Africa) and RJ Tucker (Australia)

Kenya innings		R	M	B	4s	6s	SR
AA Obanda	lbw b Southee	6	27	19	0	0	31.57
SR Waters	lbw b Bennett	16	49	42	1	0	38.09
CO Obuya	lbw b Bennett	14	32	19	2	0	73.68
SO Tikolo	b Bennett	2	4	2	0	0	100.00
MA Ouma†	lbw b Bennett	1	12	6	0	0	16.66
RR Patel	not out	16	46	23	1	0	69.56
JK Kamande*	c †BB McCullum b Oram	2	19	16	0	0	12.50
TM Odoyo	c Ryder b Oram	2	6	6	0	0	33.33
NN Odhiambo	b Southee	0	6	6	0	0	0.00
SO Ngoche	lbw b Southee	0	1	1	0	0	0.00
E Otieno	c Styris b Oram	0	4	4	0	0	0.00
Extras	(b 4, lb 3, w 2, nb 1)	10					
Total	(all out; 23.5 overs; 107 mins)	69	(2.89 runs per over)				

Fall of wickets 1-14 (Obanda, 6.6 ov), 2-40 (Waters, 11.6 ov), 3-42 (Tikolo, 13.2 ov), 4-44 (Obuya, 13.5 ov), 5-49 (Ouma, 15.3 ov), 6-59 (Kamande, 19.5 ov), 7-63 (Odoyo, 21.3 ov), 8-68 (Odhiambo, 22.5 ov), 9-68 (Ngoche, 22.6 ov), 10-69 (Otieno, 23.5 ov)

Bowling	O	M	R	W	Econ	
TG Southee	6	0	13	3	2.16	(1nb)
NL McCullum	4	0	15	0	3.75	(1w)
HK Bennett	5	0	16	4	3.20	(1w)
DL Vettori	6	1	16	0	2.66	
JDP Oram	2.5	1	2	3	0.70	

New Zealand innings		R	M	B	4s	6s	SR
MJ Guptill	not out	39	37	32	5	2	121.87
BB McCullum†	not out	26	37	17	4	0	152.94
Extras	(b 2, lb 1, w 3, nb 1)	7					
Total	(0 wickets; 8 overs; 37 mins)	72	(9.00 runs per over)				

Did not bat JD Ryder, LRPL Taylor, JEC Franklin, SB Styris, DL Vettori*, NL McCullum, JDP Oram, TG Southee, HK Bennett

Bowling	O	M	R	W	Econ	
TM Odoyo	3	0	25	0	8.33	(1w)
E Otieno	2	0	18	0	9.00	
JK Kamande	2	0	21	0	10.50	(1w)
NN Odhiambo	1	0	5	0	5.00	(1nb, 1w)

New Zealand won by 10 wickets (with 252 balls remaining)
Man of the match HK Bennett (New Zealand)

Sri Lanka vs. Canada
20 February
Mahinda Rajapaksa International Cricket Stadium, Sooriyawewa, Hambantota
Toss Sri Lanka chose to bat
Umpires IJ Gould (England) and SK Tarapore (India)

Sri Lanka innings		R	M	B	4s	6s	SR
WU Tharanga	run out (Gunasekera/†Bagai)	19	56	31	1	0	61.29
TM Dilshan	c Davison b Rizwan Cheema	50	86	59	8	0	84.74
KC Sangakkara*†	c & b Davison	92	134	87	7	1	105.74
DPMD Jayawardene	c Balaji Rao b Davison	100	115	81	9	1	123.45
NLTC Perera	run out (Surkari/†Bagai)	11	17	11	1	0	100.00
AD Mathews	c & b Baidwan	21	25	16	3	0	131.25
CK Kapugedera	c sub (NR Kumar) b Baidwan	2	5	3	0	0	66.66
TT Samaraweera	not out	18	9	10	3	0	180.00
KMDN Kulasekara	not out	7	7	3	1	0	233.33
Extras	(lb 3, w 8, nb 1)	12					
Total	(7 wickets; 50 overs; 236 mins)	332	(6.64 runs per over)				

Did not bat M Muralitharan, BAW Mendis
Fall of wickets 1-63 (Tharanga, 11.5 ov), 2-88 (Dilshan, 19.1 ov), 3-267 (Sangakkara, 41.6 ov), 4-276 (Jayawardene, 43.6 ov), 5-284 (Perera, 45.1 ov), 6-295 (Kapugedera, 46.1 ov), 7-314 (Mathews, 48.4 ov)

Bowling	O	M	R	W	Econ	
Khurram Chohan	8	0	62	0	7.75	
H Osinde	2.1	0	10	0	4.61	(1nb, 2w)
HS Baidwan	8.5	0	59	2	6.67	(2w)
AS Hansra	9	0	47	0	5.22	(1w)
Rizwan Cheema	7	0	47	1	6.71	
WD Balaji Rao	7	0	48	0	6.85	
JM Davison	8	0	56	2	7.00	(2w)

Canada innings		R	M	B	4s	6s	SR
R Gunasekera	c Dilshan b Kulasekara	1	12	10	0	0	10.00
JM Davison	b Perera	0	4	1	0	0	0.00
ZE Surkari	lbw b Perera	6	12	10	0	0	60.00
AS Hansra	st †Sangakkara b Samaraweera	9	46	49	0	0	18.36
A Bagai*†	c †Sangakkara b Perera	22	58	47	2	0	46.80
Rizwan Cheema	c Jayawardene b Muralitharan	37	65	35	4	2	105.71
TG Gordon	c †Sangakkara b Kulasekara	4	16	10	0	0	40.00
Khurram Chohan	c †Sangakkara b Kulasekara	4	11	8	1	0	50.00
HS Baidwan	not out	16	43	35	1	0	45.71
WD Balaji Rao	c Tharanga b Muralitharan	6	7	7	1	0	85.71
H Osinde	b Mendis	4	14	10	0	0	40.00
Extras	(lb 8, w 4, nb 1)	13					
Total	(all out; 36.5 overs; 148 mins)	122	(3.31 runs per over)				

Fall of wickets 1-0 (Davison, 1.1 ov), 2-8 (Gunasekera, 2.5 ov), 3-12 (Surkari, 3.6 ov), 4-42 (Hansra, 17.5 ov), 5-53 (Bagai, 21.3 ov), 6-68 (Gordon, 24.3 ov), 7-74 (Khurram Chohan, 26.2 ov), 8-103 (Rizwan Cheema, 31.3 ov), 9-111 (Balaji Rao, 33.2 ov), 10-122 (Osinde, 36.5 ov)

Bowling	O	M	R	W	Econ	
KMDN Kulasekara	6	2	16	3	2.66	
NLTC Perera	7	0	24	3	3.42	
BAW Mendis	7.5	3	18	1	2.29	(1w)
M Muralitharan	9	0	38	2	4.22	(1nb, 3w)
TM Dilshan	5	0	14	0	2.80	
TT Samaraweera	2	0	4	1	2.00	

Sri Lanka won by 210 runs
Man of the match DPMD Jayawardene (Sri Lanka)

Australia vs. Zimbabwe
21 February
Sardar Patel Stadium, Motera, Ahmedabad
Toss Australia chose to bat
Umpires EAR de Silva (Sri Lanka) and RA Kettleborough (England)

Australia innings		R	M	B	4s	6s	SR
SR Watson	lbw b Cremer	79	113	92	8	1	85.86
BJ Haddin†	lbw b Utseya	29	68	66	3	0	43.93
RT Ponting*	run out (Mpofu)	28	50	36	0	0	77.77
MJ Clarke	not out	58	77	55	4	0	105.45
CL White	b Mpofu	22	44	36	0	0	61.11
DJ Hussey	b Price	14	15	8	1	1	175.00
SPD Smith	c Chakabva b Mpofu	11	4	4	1	1	275.00
MG Johnson	not out	7	5	3	1	0	233.33
Extras	(lb 7, w 7)	14					
Total	(6 wickets; 50 overs; 191 mins)	262	(5.24 runs per over)				

Did not bat SW Tait, JJ Krejza, B Lee
Fall of wickets 1-61 (Haddin, 18.5 ov), 2-140 (Watson, 31.2 ov), 3-144 (Ponting, 32.5 ov), 4-207 (White, 44.6 ov), 5-241 (Hussey, 48.1 ov), 6-254 (Smith, 49.1 ov)

Bowling	O	M	R	W	Econ	
CB Mpofu	9	0	58	2	6.44	(2w)
RW Price	10	0	43	1	4.30	(1w)
P Utseya	10	2	43	1	4.30	(2w)
AG Cremer	10	0	41	1	4.10	(1w)
BRM Taylor	3	0	23	0	7.66	
E Chigumbura	2	0	18	0	9.00	(1w)
SC Williams	6	0	29	0	4.83	

Zimbabwe innings		R	M	B	4s	6s	SR
BRM Taylor	b Tait	16	53	24	1	0	66.66
CK Coventry	c & b Lee	14	24	24	1	1	58.33
T Taibu†	c Watson b Johnson	7	23	17	1	0	41.17
CR Ervine	lbw b Johnson	0	13	6	0	0	0.00
E Chigumbura*	c †Haddin b Krejza	14	44	25	2	0	56.00
SC Williams	c Watson b Tait	28	40	40	1	1	70.00
RW Chakabva	lbw b Krejza	6	21	18	0	0	33.33
P Utseya	c Ponting b Hussey	24	52	45	1	0	53.33
AG Cremer	c †Haddin b Johnson	37	51	51	4	0	72.54
RW Price	not out	5	25	19	0	0	26.31
CB Mpofu	c †Haddin b Johnson	2	12	11	0	0	18.18
Extras	(b 4, lb 9, w 3, nb 2)	18					
Total	(all out; 46.2 overs; 190 mins)	171	(3.69 runs per over)				

Fall of wickets 1-22 (Coventry, 5.4 ov), 2-40 (Taibu, 10.3 ov), 3-40 (Taylor, 11.2 ov), 4-44 (Ervine, 12.3 ov), 5-88 (Chigumbura, 21.2 ov), 6-96 (Williams, 24.6 ov), 7-104 (Chakabva, 27.2 ov), 8-153 (Utseya, 39.2 ov), 9-167 (Cremer, 42.4 ov), 10-171 (Mpofu, 46.2 ov)

Bowling	O	M	R	W	Econ	
SW Tait	9	1	34	2	3.77	(1nb, 2w)
B Lee	8	1	34	1	4.25	(1nb, 1w)
MG Johnson	9.2	2	19	4	2.03	
JJ Krejza	8	0	28	2	3.50	
SR Watson	3	0	7	0	2.33	
SPD Smith	5	0	24	0	4.80	
DJ Hussey	4	1	12	1	3.00	

Australia won by 91 runs
Man of the match SR Watson (Australia)

England vs. Netherlands
22 February
Vidarbha Cricket Association Stadium, Jamtha, Nagpur
Toss Netherlands chose to bat
Umpires Asad Rauf (Pakistan) and BNJ Oxenford (Australia)

Netherlands innings		R	M	B	4s	6s	SR
AN Kervezee	c †Prior b Bresnan	16	25	25	2	0	64.00
W Barresi†	st †Prior b Swann	29	49	25	6	0	116.00
TLW Cooper	c Anderson b Collingwood	47	84	73	3	0	64.38
RN ten Doeschate	c Bopara b Broad	119	160	110	9	3	108.18
B Zuiderent	c Collingwood b Swann	1	19	10	0	0	10.00
TN de Grooth	b Broad	28	47	31	3	0	90.32
PW Borren*	not out	35	41	24	4	0	145.83
Mudassar Bukhari	not out	6	11	5	0	0	120.00
Extras	(b 3, lb 3, w 2, nb 3)	11					
Total	(6 wickets; 50 overs; 224 mins)	292	(5.84 runs per over)				

Did not bat PM Seelaar, BP Loots, BA Westdijk
Fall of wickets 1-36 (Kervezee, 6.2 ov), 2-58 (Barresi, 11.4 ov), 3-136 (Cooper, 28.1 ov), 4-149 (Zuiderent, 32.5 ov), 5-213 (de Grooth, 42.5 ov), 6-274 (ten Doeschate, 48.1 ov)

Bowling	O	M	R	W	Econ	
JM Anderson	10	0	72	0	7.20	(2nb)
SCJ Broad	10	2	65	2	6.50	(1nb, 1w)
TT Bresnan	10	0	49	1	4.90	(1w)
GP Swann	10	0	35	2	3.50	
PD Collingwood	8	0	46	1	5.75	
KP Pietersen	2	0	19	0	9.50	

England innings		R	M	B	4s	6s	SR
AJ Strauss*	c Cooper b Mudassar Bukhari	88	113	83	9	0	106.02
KP Pietersen	c Borren b Seelaar	39	70	61	5	0	63.93
IJL Trott	st †Barresi b ten Doeschate	62	91	65	4	0	95.38
IR Bell	b ten Doeschate	33	61	40	1	0	82.50
PD Collingwood	not out	30	40	23	3	0	130.43
RS Bopara	not out	30	27	20	2	1	150.00
Extras	(b 1, lb 2, w 11)	14					
Total	(4 wickets; 48.4 overs; 205 mins)	296	(6.08 runs per over)				

Did not bat MJ Prior†, TT Bresnan, SCJ Broad, GP Swann, JM Anderson
Fall of wickets 1-105 (Pietersen, 17.4 ov), 2-166 (Strauss, 29.2 ov), 3-224 (Trott, 40.1 ov), 4-241 (Bell, 42.6 ov)

Bowling	O	M	R	W	Econ	
Mudassar Bukhari	9	0	54	1	6.00	
BA Westdijk	7	0	41	0	5.85	
BP Loots	9.4	0	74	0	7.65	(2w)
PM Seelaar	10	0	54	1	5.40	(2w)
RN ten Doeschate	10	0	47	2	4.70	(1w)
TLW Cooper	3	0	23	0	7.66	

England won by 6 wickets (with 8 balls remaining)
Man of the match RN ten Doeschate (Netherlands)

Kenya vs. Pakistan
23 February
Mahinda Rajapaksa International Cricket Stadium, Sooriyawewa, Hambantota
Toss Pakistan chose to bat
Umpires AL H.ill (New Zealand) and NJ Llong (England)

Pakistan innings		R	M	B	4s	6s	SR
Mohammad Hafeez	c Waters b Otieno	9	24	20	1	0	45.00
Ahmed Shehzad	c Kamande b Odoyo	1	32	18	0	0	5.55
Kamran Akmal†	st †Ouma b Ngoche	55	84	67	5	0	82.08
Younis Khan	lbw b Tikolo	50	112	67	2	0	74.62
Misbah-ul-Haq	c Otieno b Kamande	65	92	69	1	2	94.20
Umar Akmal	c Obuya b Odoyo	71	66	52	8	1	136.53
Shahid Afridi*	lbw b Odoyo	7	12	4	1	0	175.00
Abdul Razzaq	not out	8	13	6	1	0	133.33
Abdur Rehman	not out	5	10	3	0	0	166.66
Extras	(lb 3, w 37, nb 6)	46					
Total	(7 wickets; 50 overs; 226 mins)	317	(6.34 runs per over)				

Did not bat Umar Gul, Shoaib Akhtar
Fall of wickets 1-11 (Mohammad Hafeez, 5.3 ov), 2-12 (Ahmed Shehzad, 6.5 ov), 3-110 (Kamran Akmal, 24.4 ov), 4-155 (Younis Khan, 33.4 ov), 5-273 (Misbah-ul-Haq, 46.5 ov), 6-289 (Umar Akmal, 48.2 ov), 7-289 (Shahid Afridi, 48.3 ov)

Bowling	O	M	R	W	Econ	
TM Odoyo	7	2	41	3	5.85	(5w)
E Otieno	9	1	49	1	5.44	(2nb)
NN Odhiambo	7	0	65	0	9.28	(3nb, 3w)
SO Ngoche	10	0	46	1	4.60	(1w)
JK Kamande	7	0	64	1	9.14	(4w)
SO Tikolo	9	0	44	1	4.88	(1nb)
CO Obuya	1	0	5	0	5.00	

Kenya innings		R	M	B	4s	6s	SR
MA Ouma†	c †Kamran Akmal b Umar Gul	16	55	37	1	0	43.24
SR Waters	run out (Umar Akmal)	17	38	31	2	0	54.83
CO Obuya	c Ahmed Shehzad b Shahid Afridi	47	89	58	3	3	81.03
SO Tikolo	b Shahid Afridi	13	37	33	1	0	39.39
T Mishra	lbw b Shahid Afridi	6	11	16	1	0	37.50
RR Patel	c Umar Akmal b Mohammad Hafeez	0	4	6	0	0	0.00
JK Kamande*	lbw b Shahid Afridi	2	3	3	0	0	66.66
TM Odoyo	lbw b Shahid Afridi	0	8	8	0	0	0.00
NN Odhiambo	run out (sub [Asad Shafiq])	0	8	6	0	0	0.00
SO Ngoche	b Umar Gul	0	8	1	0	0	0.00
E Otieno	not out	0	3	1	0	0	0.00
Extras	(b 4, lb 3, w 3, nb 1)	11					
Total	(all out; 33.1 overs; 136 mins)	112	(3.37 runs per over)				

Fall of wickets 1-37 (Waters, 9.1 ov), 2-43 (Ouma, 12.2 ov), 3-73 (Tikolo, 22.2 ov), 4-79 (Mishra, 26.3 ov), 5-85 (Patel, 27.5 ov), 6-87 (Kamande, 28.3 ov), 7-101 (Odoyo, 30.5 ov), 8-112 (Obuya, 32.1 ov), 9-112 (Odhiambo, 32.5 ov), 10-112 (Ngoche, 33.1 ov)

Bowling	O	M	R	W	Econ	
Shoaib Akhtar	5	1	10	0	2.00	(1w)
Abdul Razzaq	5	1	23	0	4.60	
Umar Gul	4.1	0	12	2	2.88	(1nb, 1w)
Abdur Rehman	7	1	18	0	2.57	
Shahid Afridi	8	3	16	5	2.00	
Mohammad Hafeez	4	1	26	1	6.50	(1w)

Pakistan won by 205 runs
Man of the match Umar Akmal (Pakistan)

South Africa vs. West Indies
24 February
Feroz Shah Kotla, Delhi
Toss South Africa chose to field
Umpires AM Saheba and SJA Taufel (Australia)

West Indies innings		R	M	B	4s	6s	SR
CH Gayle	c Kallis b Botha	2	3	3	0	0	66.66
DS Smith	c & b Imran Tahir	36	103	57	3	0	63.15
DM Bravo	lbw b Botha	73	96	82	8	1	89.02
RR Sarwan	lbw b Imran Tahir	2	15	10	0	0	20.00
S Chanderpaul	c Peterson b Imran Tahir	31	73	51	1	1	60.78
DJ Bravo	run out (Morkel/†de Villiers)	40	46	37	1	3	108.10
DC Thomas†	c Duminy b Imran Tahir	15	29	26	1	0	57.69
KA Pollard	lbw b Steyn	0	6	1	0	0	0.00
DJG Sammy*	lbw b Steyn	0	7	4	0	0	0.00
SJ Benn	c Morkel b Steyn	6	14	8	1	0	75.00
KAJ Roach	not out	2	12	6	0	0	33.33
Extras	(b 1, lb 3, w 11)	15					
Total	(all out; 47.3 overs; 205 mins)	222	(4.67 runs per over)				

Fall of wickets 1-2 (Gayle, 0.3 ov), 2-113 (DM Bravo, 23.1 ov), 3-117 (Smith, 24.4 ov), 4-120 (Sarwan, 26.1 ov), 5-178 (DJ Bravo, 37.5 ov), 6-209 (Chanderpaul, 42.2 ov), 7-213 (Pollard, 43.3 ov), 8-213 (Thomas, 44.6 ov), 9-213 (Sammy, 45.1 ov), 10-222 (Benn, 47.3 ov)

Bowling	O	M	R	W	Econ	
J Botha	9	0	48	2	5.33	(3w)
DW Steyn	7.3	1	24	3	3.20	(2w)
M Morkel	8	0	35	0	4.37	(2w)
JH Kallis	3	0	21	0	7.00	
Imran Tahir	10	1	41	4	4.10	
RJ Peterson	10	0	49	0	4.90	

South Africa innings		R	M	B	4s	6s	SR
HM Amla	c †Thomas b Roach	14	14	15	2	0	93.33
GC Smith*	b Pollard	45	116	78	2	0	57.69
JH Kallis	c Sammy b Benn	4	5	7	0	0	57.14
AB de Villiers†	not out	107	149	105	8	2	101.90
JP Duminy	not out	42	54	53	1	0	79.24
Extras	(lb 10, nb 1)	11					
Total	(3 wickets; 42.5 overs; 171 mins)	223	(5.20 runs per over)				

Did not bat F du Plessis, J Botha, RJ Peterson, M Morkel, DW Steyn, Imran Tahir
Fall of wickets 1-15 (Amla, 3.3 ov), 2-20 (Kallis, 4.6 ov), 3-139 (Smith, 28.3 ov)

Bowling	O	M	R	W	Econ	
SJ Benn	10	0	51	1	5.10	
KAJ Roach	8	0	42	1	5.25	
DJ Bravo	2.1	0	12	0	5.53	
DJG Sammy	8	0	40	0	5.00	
KA Pollard	7.5	0	37	1	4.72	(1nb)
CH Gayle	6	0	26	0	4.33	
DS Smith	0.5	0	5	0	6.00	

South Africa won by 7 wickets (with 43 balls remaining)
Man of the match AB de Villiers (South Africa)

Australia vs. New Zealand
25 February
Vidarbha Cricket Association Stadium, Jamtha, Nagpur
Toss Australia chose to field
Umpires HDPK Dharmasena (Sri Lanka) and BR Doctrove (West Indies)

New Zealand innings		R	M	B	4s	6s	SR
MJ Guptill	b Watson	10	45	25	2	0	40.00
BB McCullum†	c Krejza b Tait	16	19	12	3	0	133.33
JD Ryder	c †Haddin b Johnson	25	49	31	6	0	80.64
LRPL Taylor	b Tait	7	45	22	1	0	31.81
JEC Franklin	c †Haddin b Johnson	0	2	3	0	0	0.00
SB Styris	c †Haddin b Tait	0	4	4	0	0	0.00
JM How	lbw b Smith	22	60	47	1	0	46.80
NL McCullum	lbw b Johnson	52	94	76	3	0	68.42
DL Vettori*	c †Haddin b Lee	44	62	43	5	0	102.32
TG Southee	c Ponting b Johnson	6	20	10	0	0	60.00
HK Bennett	not out	0	1	0	0	0	-
Extras	(b 1, lb 8, w 13, nb 2)	24					
Total	(all out; 45.1 overs; 207 mins)	206	(4.56 runs per over)				

Fall of wickets 1-20 (BB McCullum, 3.4 ov), 2-40 (Guptill, 8.5 ov), 3-66 (Ryder, 13.2 ov), 4-66 (Franklin, 13.5 ov), 5-67 (Styris, 14.4 ov), 6-73 (Taylor, 16.6 ov), 7-121 (How, 28.6 ov), 8-175 (NL McCullum, 41.2 ov), 9-206 (Vettori, 44.6 ov), 10-206 (Southee, 45.1 ov)

Bowling	O	M	R	W	Econ	
B Lee	8	2	29	1	3.62	
SW Tait	7	0	35	3	5.00	(2nb, 4w)
MG Johnson	9.1	3	33	4	3.60	(2w)
SR Watson	3	1	9	1	3.00	(1w)
JJ Krejza	9	0	47	0	5.22	(1w)
SPD Smith	9	0	44	1	4.88	(1w)

Australia innings		R	M	B	4s	6s	SR
SR Watson	b Bennett	62	87	61	6	1	101.63
BJ Haddin†	c Franklin b Bennett	55	84	50	8	0	110.00
RT Ponting*	st †BB McCullum b Southee	12	39	28	1	0	42.85
MJ Clarke	not out	24	77	37	4	0	64.86
CL White	not out	22	39	28	3	0	78.57
Extras	(lb 3, w 29)	32					
Total	(3 wickets; 34 overs; 167 mins)	207	(6.08 runs per over)				

Did not bat DJ Hussey, SPD Smith, MG Johnson, JJ Krejza, B Lee, SW Tait
Fall of wickets 1-133 (Haddin, 18.1 ov), 2-136 (Watson, 18.3 ov), 3-167 (Ponting, 26.4 ov)

Bowling	O	M	R	W	Econ	
TG Southee	10	2	45	1	4.50	(4w)
DL Vettori	7	0	39	0	5.57	(1w)
HK Bennett	7	0	63	2	9.00	(7w)
NL McCullum	3	0	22	0	7.33	
JD Ryder	5	0	24	0	4.80	(3w)
JEC Franklin	2	0	11	0	5.50	

Australia won by 7 wickets (with 96 balls remaining)
Man of the match MG Johnson (Australia)

Bangladesh v Ireland

25 February
Shere Bangla National Stadium, Mirpur
Toss Bangladesh chose to bat
Umpires Aleem Dar (Pakistan) and RJ Tucker (Australia)

Bangladesh innings		R	M	B	4s	6s	SR
Tamim Iqbal	c Porterfield b Botha	44	52	43	7	0	102.32
Imrul Kayes	st †NJ O'Brien b Mooney	12	29	12	2	0	100.00
Junaid Siddique	run out (Joyce)	3	9	8	0	0	37.50
Mushfiqur Rahim†	c White b Dockrell	36	95	66	2	0	54.54
Shakib Al Hasan*	c & b Botha	16	17	20	3	0	80.00
Raqibul Hasan	run out (White)	38	87	69	1	0	55.07
Mohammad Ashraful	c White b Dockrell	1	9	6	0	0	16.66
Naeem Islam	c Dockrell b Johnston	29	64	38	3	0	76.31
Shafiul Islam	lbw b Botha	2	14	17	0	0	11.76
Abdur Razzak	b Johnston	11	28	16	0	0	68.75
Rubel Hossain	not out	2	7	2	0	0	100.00
Extras	(b 2, w 8, nb 1)	11					
Total	(all out; 49.2 overs)	205	(4.15 runs per over)				

Fall of wickets 1-53 (Imrul Kayes, 6.3 ov), 2-61 (Junaid Siddique, 8.5 ov), 3-68 (Tamim Iqbal, 11.1 ov), 4-86 (Shakib Al Hasan, 15.2 ov), 5-147 (Mushfiqur Rahim, 33.3 ov), 6-151 (Mohammad Ashraful, 35.2 ov), 7-159 (Raqibul Hasan, 38.1 ov), 8-170 (Shafiul Islam, 42.3 ov), 9-193 (Abdur Razzak, 47.6 ov), 10-205 (Naeem Islam, 49.2 ov)

Bowling	O	M	R	W	Econ	
WB Rankin	9	0	62	0	6.88	(4w)
DT Johnston	8.2	0	40	2	4.80	(1nb)
JF Mooney	7	0	25	1	3.57	(1w)
AC Botha	9	1	32	3	3.55	(1w)
GH Dockrell	10	2	23	2	2.30	
PR Stirling	4	0	13	0	3.25	
KJ O'Brien	2	0	8	0	4.00	

Ireland innings		R	M	B	4s	6s	SR
WTS Porterfield*	c Raqibul Hasan b Shakib Al Hasan	20	31	30	2	0	66.66
PR Stirling	st †Mushfiqur Rahim b Abdur Razzak	9	18	10	1	0	90.00
EC Joyce	c & b Mohammad Ashraful	16	45	35	0	0	45.71
NJ O'Brien†	c Tamim Iqbal b Shakib Al Hasan	38	64	52	3	0	73.07
AR White	b Mohammad Ashraful	10	20	27	1	0	37.03
KJ O'Brien	c sub (Suhrawadi Shuvo) b Shafiul Islam	37	46	40	3	1	92.50
AC Botha	b Shafiul Islam	22	55	36	2	0	61.11
JF Mooney	b Naeem Islam	0	16	8	0	0	0.00
DT Johnston	lbw b Shafiul Islam	6	10	6	1	0	100.00
GH Dockrell	not out	4	21	12	0	0	33.33
WB Rankin	c Junaid Siddique b Shafiul Islam	3	12	13	0	0	23.07
Extras	(lb 9, w 4)	13					
Total	(all out; 45 overs)	178	(3.95 runs per over)				

Fall of wickets 1-23 (Stirling, 5.3 ov), 2-36 (Porterfield, 9.1 ov), 3-75 (Joyce, 18.1 ov), 4-93 (White, 24.4 ov), 5-110 (NJ O'Brien, 27.4 ov), 6-151 (KJ O'Brien, 36.4 ov), 7-164 (Mooney, 39.4 ov), 8-168 (Botha, 40.1 ov), 9-171 (Johnston, 42.1 ov), 10-178 (Rankin, 44.6 ov)

Bowling	O	M	R	W	Econ	
Shafiul Islam	8	1	21	4	2.62	(2w)
Abdur Razzak	8	0	30	1	3.75	
Naeem Islam	9	1	36	1	4.00	
Shakib Al Hasan	8	0	28	2	3.50	(1w)
Mohammad Ashraful	9	0	42	2	4.66	(1w)
Rubel Hossain	3	0	12	0	4.00	

Bangladesh won by 27 runs
Man of the match Tamim Iqbal (Bangladesh)

Sri Lanka vs. Pakistan
26 February
R Premadasa Stadium, Colombo
Toss Pakistan chose to bat
Umpires IJ Gould (England) and DJ Harper (Australia)

Pakistan innings		R	M	B	4s	6s	SR
Ahmed Shehzad	c †Sangakkara b Perera	13	24	23	2	0	56.52
Mohammad Hafeez	run out (Jayawardene/†Sangakkara/Herath)	32	63	31	4	1	103.22
Kamran Akmal†	st †Sangakkara b Herath	39	68	48	5	0	81.25
Younis Khan	c Jayawardene b Herath	72	108	76	4	0	94.73
Misbah-ul-Haq	not out	83	118	91	6	0	91.20
Umar Akmal	c Dilshan b Muralitharan	10	21	15	1	0	66.66
Shahid Afridi*	c Dilshan b Mathews	16	18	12	3	0	133.33
Abdul Razzaq	c sub (CK Kapugedera) b Perera	3	6	4	0	0	75.00
Extras	(lb 4, w 5)	9					
Total	(7 wickets; 50 overs; 220 mins)	277	(5.54 runs per over)				

Did not bat Umar Gul, Abdur Rehman, Shoaib Akhtar
Fall of wickets 1-28 (Ahmed Shehzad, 5.3 ov), 2-76 (Mohammad Hafeez, 13.1 ov), 3-105 (Kamran Akmal, 20.2 ov), 4-213 (Younis Khan, 40.5 ov), 5-238 (Umar Akmal, 45.3 ov), 6-267 (Shahid Afridi, 48.5 ov), 7-277 (Abdul Razzaq, 49.6 ov)

Bowling	O	M	R	W	Econ	
KMDN Kulasekara	10	1	64	0	6.40	(1w)
NLTC Perera	9	0	62	2	6.88	(2w)
AD Mathews	10	0	56	1	5.60	
M Muralitharan	10	0	35	1	3.50	(2w)
HMRKB Herath	10	0	46	2	4.60	
TM Dilshan	1	0	10	0	10.00	

Sri Lanka innings		R	M	B	4s	6s	SR
WU Tharanga	c Shahid Afridi b Mohammad Hafeez	33	64	43	6	0	76.74
TM Dilshan	b Shahid Afridi	41	81	55	5	0	74.54
KC Sangakkara*†	c Ahmed Shehzad b Shahid Afridi	49	109	61	2	1	80.32
DPMD Jayawardene	b Shoaib Akhtar	2	12	10	0	0	20.00
TT Samaraweera	st †Kamran Akmal b Shahid Afridi	1	6	4	0	0	25.00
LPC Silva	st †Kamran Akmal b Abdur Rehman	57	115	78	5	0	73.07
AD Mathews	c Ahmed Shehzad b Shahid Afridi	18	24	20	2	0	90.00
NLTC Perera	b Shoaib Akhtar	8	14	6	1	0	133.33
KMDN Kulasekara	c Umar Akmal b Umar Gul	24	21	14	2	1	171.42
HMRKB Herath	not out	4	20	10	0	0	40.00
M Muralitharan	not out	0	1	1	0	0	0.00
Extras	(b 1, lb 10, w 16, nb 2)	29					
Total	(9 wickets; 50 overs; 238 mins)	266	(5.32 runs per over)				

Fall of wickets 1-76 (Tharanga, 14.2 ov), 2-88 (Dilshan, 17.3 ov), 3-95 (Jayawardene, 20.2 ov), 4-96 (Samaraweera, 21.2 ov), 5-169 (Sangakkara, 37.4 ov), 6-209 (Mathews, 43.4 ov), 7-232 (Perera, 45.5 ov), 8-233 (Silva, 46.0 ov), 9-265 (Kulasekara, 49.5 ov)

Bowling	O	M	R	W	Econ	
Shoaib Akhtar	10	0	42	2	4.20	
Abdul Razzaq	5	1	23	0	4.60	
Umar Gul	9	0	60	1	6.66	(1nb, 2w)
Mohammad Hafeez	6	0	33	1	5.50	(2w)
Shahid Afridi	10	0	34	4	3.40	(1w)
Abdur Rehman	10	1	63	1	6.30	(1nb, 3w)

Pakistan won by 11 runs
Man of the match Shahid Afridi (Pakistan)

India vs. England
27 February
M Chinnaswamy Stadium, Bangalore
Toss India chose to bat
Umpires BF Bowden (New Zealand) and M Erasmus (South Africa)

India innings		R	M	B	4s	6s	SR
V Sehwag	c †Prior b Bresnan	35	34	26	6	0	134.61
SR Tendulkar	c Yardy b Anderson	120	170	115	10	5	104.34
G Gambhir	b Swann	51	95	61	5	0	83.60
Yuvraj Singh	c Bell b Yardy	58	76	50	9	0	116.00
MS Dhoni*†	c sub (LJ Wright) b Bresnan	31	38	25	3	1	124.00
YK Pathan	c Swann b Bresnan	14	12	8	1	1	175.00
V Kohli	b Bresnan	8	12	5	1	0	160.00
Harbhajan Singh	lbw b Bresnan	0	4	1	0	0	0.00
Z Khan	run out (Bresnan/†Prior)	4	10	5	0	0	80.00
PP Chawla	run out (Anderson)	2	5	4	0	0	50.00
MM Patel	not out	0	1	0	0	0	-
Extras	(lb 3, w 7, nb 5)	15					
Total	(all out; 49.5 overs; 233 mins)	338	(6.78 runs per over)				

Fall of wickets 1-46 (Sehwag, 7.5 ov), 2-180 (Gambhir, 29.4 ov), 3-236 (Tendulkar, 38.2 ov), 4-305 (Yuvraj Singh, 45.6 ov), 5-305 (Dhoni, 46.1 ov), 6-327 (Pathan, 48.1 ov), 7-327 (Kohli, 48.2 ov), 8-328 (Harbhajan Singh, 48.4 ov), 9-338 (Chawla, 49.4 ov), 10-338 (Khan, 49.5 ov)

Bowling	O	M	R	W	Econ	
JM Anderson	9.5	0	91	1	9.25	(1nb, 1w)
A Shahzad	8	0	53	0	6.62	(2w)
TT Bresnan	10	1	48	5	4.80	
GP Swann	9	1	59	1	6.55	(2w)
PD Collingwood	3	0	20	0	6.66	
MH Yardy	10	0	64	1	6.40	(2w)

England innings		R	M	B	4s	6s	SR
AJ Strauss*	lbw b Khan	158	188	145	18	1	108.96
KP Pietersen	c & b Patel	31	45	22	5	0	140.90
IJL Trott	lbw b Chawla	16	30	19	1	0	84.21
IR Bell	c Kohli b Khan	69	108	71	4	1	97.18
PD Collingwood	b Khan	1	12	5	0	0	20.00
MJ Prior†	c sub (SK Raina) b Harbhajan Singh	4	15	8	0	0	50.00
MH Yardy	c Sehwag b Patel	13	17	10	1	0	130.00
TT Bresnan	b Chawla	14	18	9	0	1	155.55
GP Swann	not out	15	12	9	0	1	166.66
A Shahzad	not out	6	5	2	0	1	300.00
Extras	(b 1, lb 7, w 3)	11					
Total	(8 wickets; 50 overs; 229 mins)	338	(6.76 runs per over)				

Did not bat JM Anderson
Fall of wickets 1-68 (Pietersen, 9.3 ov), 2-111 (Trott, 16.4 ov), 3-281 (Bell, 42.4 ov), 4-281 (Strauss, 42.5 ov), 5-285 (Collingwood, 44.3 ov), 6-289 (Prior, 45.2 ov), 7-307 (Yardy, 47.3 ov), 8-325 (Bresnan, 48.6 ov)

Bowling	O	M	R	W	Econ	
Z Khan	10	0	64	3	6.40	(1w)
MM Patel	10	0	70	2	7.00	(1w)
PP Chawla	10	0	71	2	7.10	(1w)
Harbhajan Singh	10	0	58	1	5.80	
Yuvraj Singh	7	0	46	0	6.57	
YK Pathan	3	0	21	0	7.00	

Match tied
Man of the match AJ Strauss (England)

Canada vs. Zimbabwe
28 February
Vidarbha Cricket Association Stadium, Jamtha, Nagpur
Toss Zimbabwe chose to bat
Umpires Asad Rauf (Pakistan) and BNJ Oxenford (Australia)

Zimbabwe innings		R	M	B	4s	6s	SR
BRM Taylor	lbw b Khurram Chohan	0	1	1	0	0	0.00
CK Coventry	lbw b Baidwan	4	16	10	0	0	40.00
T Taibu†	c Davison b Balaji Rao	98	147	99	9	0	98.98
CR Ervine	c †Bagai b Balaji Rao	85	114	81	6	2	104.93
E Chigumbura*	c †Bagai b Rizwan Cheema	5	6	8	1	0	62.50
SC Williams	c †Bagai b Balaji Rao	30	34	25	3	0	120.00
GA Lamb	b Balaji Rao	11	12	13	1	0	84.61
P Utseya	c Hansra b Khurram Chohan	22	40	29	2	0	75.86
AG Cremer	b Baidwan	26	31	23	2	0	113.04
RW Price	not out	10	14	6	2	0	166.66
CB Mpofu	not out	3	9	5	0	0	60.00
Extras	(lb 2, w 1, nb 1)	4					
Total	(9 wickets; 50 overs; 219 mins)	298	(5.96 runs per over)				

Fall of wickets 1-0 (Taylor, 0.1 ov), 2-7 (Coventry, 3.3 ov), 3-188 (Ervine, 31.2 ov), 4-193 (Chigumbura, 32.4 ov), 5-201 (Taibu, 33.6 ov), 6-219 (Lamb, 37.4 ov), 7-240 (Williams, 41.4 ov), 8-281 (Utseya, 47.4 ov), 9-284 (Cremer, 48.2 ov)

Bowling	O	M	R	W	Econ	
Khurram Chohan	10	0	44	2	4.40	(1nb, 1w)
HS Baidwan	9	0	47	2	5.22	
AS Hansra	4	0	41	0	10.25	
Rizwan Cheema	9	0	51	1	5.66	
WD Balaji Rao	10	0	57	4	5.70	
JM Davison	8	0	56	0	7.00	

Canada innings		R	M	B	4s	6s	SR
JM Davison	b Price	0	5	8	0	0	0.00
NR Kumar	c & b Price	1	22	10	0	0	10.00
R Gunasekera	b Lamb	24	76	64	2	0	37.50
A Bagai*†	c Williams b Price	0	1	1	0	0	0.00
AS Hansra	st †Taibu b Utseya	20	53	41	1	1	48.78
Rizwan Cheema	c Cremer b Utseya	14	9	10	2	1	140.00
ZE Surkari	st †Taibu b Lamb	26	70	48	2	0	54.16
TG Gordon	lbw b Cremer	7	13	20	1	0	35.00
Khurram Chohan	lbw b Cremer	8	22	22	1	0	36.36
HS Baidwan	not out	13	29	23	1	0	56.52
WD Balaji Rao	b Cremer	1	3	6	0	0	16.66
Extras	(w 9)	9					
Total	(all out; 42.1 overs; 160 mins)	123	(2.91 runs per over)				

Fall of wickets 1-1 (Davison, 1.3 ov), 2-7 (Kumar, 5.3 ov), 3-7 (Bagai, 5.4 ov), 4-50 (Hansra, 20.3 ov), 5-50 (Gunasekera, 21.1 ov), 6-66 (Rizwan Cheema, 22.5 ov), 7-78 (Gordon, 26.6 ov), 8-97 (Khurram Chohan, 34.3 ov), 9-122 (Surkari, 41.1 ov), 10-123 (Balaji Rao, 42.1 ov)

Bowling	O	M	R	W	Econ	
CB Mpofu	5	1	12	0	2.40	(1w)
RW Price	8	4	16	3	2.00	
P Utseya	7	0	24	2	3.42	(2w)
GA Lamb	8	0	29	2	3.62	(6w)
AG Cremer	9.1	1	31	3	3.38	
SC Williams	5	0	11	0	2.20	

Zimbabwe won by 175 runs
Man of the match T Taibu (Zimbabwe)

Netherlands vs. West Indies
28 February
Feroz Shah Kotla, Delhi
Toss Netherlands chose to field
Umpires AM Saheba and SJA Taufel (Australia)

West Indies innings		R	M	B	4s	6s	SR
DS Smith	c †Barresi b Loots	53	67	51	9	0	103.92
CH Gayle	c Kervezee b ten Doeschate	80	136	110	7	2	72.72
DM Bravo	c Kervezee b Seelaar	30	42	38	1	2	78.94
RR Sarwan	lbw b Westdijk	49	55	42	7	1	116.66
KA Pollard	c ten Doeschate b Mudassar Bukhari	60	59	27	5	4	222.22
DJG Sammy*	c Kervezee b Seelaar	6	6	6	1	0	100.00
S Chanderpaul	b Seelaar	4	9	6	0	0	66.66
DC Thomas†	lbw b Mudassar Bukhari	13	24	13	1	0	100.00
NO Miller	not out	11	13	7	2	0	157.14
SJ Benn	not out	3	1	1	0	0	300.00
Extras	(b 3, lb 3, w 14, nb 1)	21					
Total	(8 wickets; 50 overs; 213 mins)	330	(6.60 runs per over)				

Did not bat KAJ Roach
Fall of wickets 1-100 (Smith, 16.3 ov), 2-168 (Bravo, 31.2 ov), 3-196 (Gayle, 36.2 ov), 4-261 (Sarwan, 42.1 ov), 5-278 (Sammy, 43.4 ov), 6-290 (Chanderpaul, 45.4 ov), 7-312 (Pollard, 47.5 ov), 8-326 (Thomas, 49.4 ov)

Bowling	O	M	R	W	Econ	
Mudassar Bukhari	10	1	65	2	6.50	(1w)
BA Westdijk	7	0	56	1	8.00	(4w)
RN ten Doeschate	10	0	77	1	7.70	(1nb, 4w)
BP Loots	7	0	44	1	6.28	(1w)
TLW Cooper	6	0	37	0	6.16	(1w)
PM Seelaar	10	1	45	3	4.50	

Netherlands innings		R	M	B	4s	6s	SR
AN Kervezee	st †Thomas b Benn	14	20	20	2	0	70.00
W Barresi†	c Gayle b Roach	0	4	5	0	0	0.00
TLW Cooper	not out	55	114	72	9	0	76.38
RN ten Doeschate	lbw b Benn	7	7	6	1	0	116.66
B Zuiderent	b Roach	1	5	4	0	0	25.00
TN de Grooth	lbw b Benn	1	6	5	0	0	20.00
PW Borren*	c Pollard b Sammy	10	25	28	1	0	35.71
Mudassar Bukhari	b Roach	24	35	42	2	0	57.14
PM Seelaar	lbw b Roach	1	8	5	0	0	20.00
BP Loots	lbw b Roach	0	1	1	0	0	0.00
BA Westdijk	b Roach	0	1	1	0	0	0.00
Extras	(lb 2)	2					
Total	(all out; 31.3 overs; 119 mins)	115	(3.65 runs per over)				

Fall of wickets 1-2 (Barresi, 1.4 ov), 2-26 (Kervezee, 6.4 ov), 3-34 (ten Doeschate, 8.1 ov), 4-35 (Zuiderent, 9.3 ov), 5-36 (de Grooth, 10.2 ov), 6-56 (Borren, 18.2 ov), 7-113 (Mudassar Bukhari, 29.4 ov), 8-115 (Seelaar, 31.1 ov), 9-115 (Loots, 31.2 ov), 10-115 (Westdijk, 31.3 ov)

Bowling	O	M	R	W	Econ
SJ Benn	8	1	28	3	3.50
KAJ Roach	8.3	0	27	6	3.17
NO Miller	7	0	23	0	3.28
DJG Sammy	7	0	33	1	4.71
KA Pollard	1	0	2	0	2.00

West Indies won by 215 runs
Man of the match KAJ Roach (West Indies)

Sri Lanka vs. Kenya
1 March
R Premadasa Stadium, Colombo
Toss Kenya chose to bat
Umpires AL Hill (New Zealand) and SK Tarapore (India)

Kenya innings		R	M	B	4s	6s	SR
MA Ouma†	lbw b Kulasekara	1	7	7	0	0	14.28
SR Waters	lbw b Malinga	3	12	4	0	0	75.00
CO Obuya	b Malinga	52	121	100	4	0	52.00
DO Obuya	c Samaraweera b Muralitharan	51	158	106	3	0	48.11
SO Tikolo	c Dilshan b Mathews	7	20	17	1	0	41.17
T Mishra	lbw b Malinga	0	28	13	0	0	0.00
JK Kamande*	run out (Silva)	1	4	3	0	0	33.33
NN Odhiambo	not out	8	15	10	2	0	80.00
PJ Ongondo	b Malinga	0	3	1	0	0	0.00
SO Ngoche	b Malinga	0	1	1	0	0	0.00
E Otieno	b Malinga	0	2	2	0	0	0.00
Extras	(b 1, lb 6, w 9, nb 3)	19					
Total	(all out; 43.4 overs)	142	(3.25 runs per over)				

Fall of wickets 1-4 (Ouma, 1.2 ov), 2-8 (Waters, 2.1 ov), 3-102 (CO Obuya, 31.4 ov), 4-120 (Tikolo, 36.2 ov), 5-127 (DO Obuya, 40.1 ov), 6-128 (Kamande, 41.1 ov), 7-137 (Mishra, 41.6 ov), 8-137 (Ongondo, 43.1 ov), 9-137 (Ngoche, 43.2 ov), 10-142 (Otieno, 43.4 ov)

Bowling	O	M	R	W	Econ	
SL Malinga	7.4	0	38	6	4.95	(2nb, 3w)
KMDN Kulasekara	9	1	18	1	2.00	
AD Mathews	7	0	20	1	2.85	(1w)
BAW Mendis	9	2	23	0	2.55	
M Muralitharan	8	0	24	1	3.00	
LPC Silva	3	0	12	0	4.00	(1w)

Sri Lanka innings		R	M	B	4s	6s	SR
WU Tharanga	not out	67	92	59	12	0	113.55
TM Dilshan	c †Ouma b Otieno	44	41	30	8	0	146.66
KC Sangakkara*†	not out	27	48	24	3	0	112.50
Extras	(w 7, nb 1)	8					
Total	(1 wicket; 18.4 overs; 92 mins)	146	(7.82 runs per over)				

Did not bat DPMD Jayawardene, TT Samaraweera, LPC Silva, AD Mathews, KMDN Kulasekara, M Muralitharan, SL Malinga, BAW Mendis
Fall of wickets 1-72 (Dilshan, 8.2 ov)

Bowling	O	M	R	W	Econ	
PJ Ongondo	3	0	28	0	9.33	(1w)
NN Odhiambo	5	0	26	0	5.20	
SO Ngoche	4	0	39	0	9.75	
JK Kamande	1	0	14	0	14.00	(2w)
E Otieno	4	0	26	1	6.50	(1nb, 1w)
CO Obuya	1.4	0	13	0	7.80	(1w)

Sri Lanka won by 9 wickets (with 188 balls remaining)
Man of the match SL Malinga (Sri Lanka)

England vs. Ireland
2 March
M Chinnaswamy Stadium, Bangalore
Toss England chose to bat
Umpires Aleem Dar (Pakistan) and BF Bowden (New Zealand)

England innings		R	M	B	4s	6s	SR
AJ Strauss*	b Dockrell	34	61	37	2	1	91.89
KP Pietersen	c †NJ O'Brien b Stirling	59	77	50	7	2	118.00
IJL Trott	b Mooney	92	126	92	9	0	100.00
IR Bell	c Stirling b Mooney	81	102	86	6	1	94.18
PD Collingwood	c KJ O'Brien b Mooney	16	21	11	0	1	145.45
MJ Prior†	b Johnston	6	7	5	1	0	120.00
TT Bresnan	c Johnston b Mooney	4	23	8	0	0	50.00
MH Yardy	b Johnston	3	8	6	0	0	50.00
GP Swann	not out	9	8	5	1	0	180.00
Extras	(b 1, lb 2, w 20)	23					
Total	(8 wickets; 50 overs; 220 mins)	327	(6.54 runs per over)				

Did not bat SCJ Broad, JM Anderson
Fall of wickets 1-91 (Strauss, 13.3 ov), 2-111 (Pietersen, 16.6 ov), 3-278 (Bell, 42.6 ov), 4-288 (Trott, 44.3 ov), 5-299 (Prior, 45.6 ov), 6-312 (Collingwood, 46.6 ov), 7-317 (Yardy, 48.3 ov), 8-327 (Bresnan, 49.6 ov)

Bowling	O	M	R	W	Econ	
WB Rankin	7	0	51	0	7.28	(4w)
DT Johnston	10	0	58	2	5.80	
AR Cusack	4	0	39	0	9.75	(1w)
GH Dockrell	10	0	68	1	6.80	(5w)
JF Mooney	9	0	63	4	7.00	(1w)
PR Stirling	10	0	45	1	4.50	

Ireland innings		R	M	B	4s	6s	SR
WTS Porterfield*	b Anderson	0	1	1	0	0	0.00
PR Stirling	c Pietersen b Bresnan	32	45	28	5	1	114.28
EC Joyce	st †Prior b Swann	32	90	61	3	0	52.45
NJ O'Brien†	b Swann	29	37	36	2	1	80.55
GC Wilson	lbw b Swann	3	17	14	0	0	21.42
KJ O'Brien	run out (†Prior/Bresnan)	113	123	63	13	6	179.36
AR Cusack	run out (Broad/Collingwood)	47	80	58	3	1	81.03
JF Mooney	not out	33	40	30	6	0	110.00
DT Johnston	not out	7	6	4	1	0	175.00
Extras	(b 5, lb 16, w 12)	33					
Total	(7 wickets; 49.1 overs; 223 mins)	329	(6.69 runs per over)				

Did not bat GH Dockrell, WB Rankin
Fall of wickets 1-0 (Porterfield, 0.1 ov), 2-62 (Stirling, 9.5 ov), 3-103 (NJ O'Brien, 20.2 ov), 4-106 (Joyce, 22.2 ov), 5-111 (Wilson, 24.2 ov), 6-273 (Cusack, 41.3 ov), 7-317 (KJ O'Brien, 48.1 ov)

Bowling	O	M	R	W	Econ	
JM Anderson	8.1	1	49	1	6.00	(1w)
SCJ Broad	9	0	73	0	8.11	(2w)
TT Bresnan	10	0	64	1	6.40	(2w)
MH Yardy	7	0	49	0	7.00	(2w)
GP Swann	10	0	47	3	4.70	
PD Collingwood	5	0	26	0	5.20	

Ireland won by 3 wickets (with 5 balls remaining)
Man of the match KJ O'Brien (Ireland)

Netherlands vs. South Africa

3 March
Punjab Cricket Association Stadium, Mohali, Chandigarh
Toss Netherlands chose to field
Umpires EAR de Silva (Sri Lanka) and RA Kettleborough (England)

South Africa innings		R	M	B	4s	6s	SR
HM Amla	c Cooper b ten Doeschate	113	191	130	8	0	86.92
GC Smith*	b Loots	20	57	32	1	0	62.50
JH Kallis	c †Barresi b ten Doeschate	2	10	12	0	0	16.66
AB de Villiers†	run out (Westdijk/Mudassar Bukhari)	134	126	98	13	4	136.73
F du Plessis	not out	18	27	14	1	0	128.57
JP Duminy	c Borren b ten Doeschate	40	18	15	2	4	266.66
MN van Wyk	not out	0	1	0	0	0	-
Extras	(b 2, lb 5, w 16, nb 1)	24					
Total	(5 wickets; 50 overs; 220 mins)	351	(7.02 runs per over)				

Did not bat RJ Peterson, M Morkel, DW Steyn, Imran Tahir
Fall of wickets 1-51 (Smith, 12.5 ov), 2-58 (Kallis, 15.3 ov), 3-279 (Amla, 44.5 ov), 4-283 (de Villiers, 45.4 ov), 5-349 (Duminy, 49.5 ov)

Bowling	O	M	R	W	Econ	
Mudassar Bukhari	10	0	44	0	4.40	(2w)
BA Westdijk	9	0	76	0	8.44	(4w)
RN ten Doeschate	10	0	72	3	7.20	(1w)
BP Loots	9	0	60	1	6.66	(1nb)
PM Seelaar	10	0	74	0	7.40	
TLW Cooper	2	0	18	0	9.00	

Netherlands innings		R	M	B	4s	6s	SR
AN Kervezee	c & b Kallis	10	23	18	1	0	55.55
W Barresi†	st †van Wyk b Duminy	44	98	66	5	0	66.66
TLW Cooper	c Steyn b Kallis	9	26	21	1	0	42.85
B Zuiderent	lbw b Peterson	15	38	26	1	1	57.69
RN ten Doeschate	lbw b Steyn	11	23	21	0	0	52.38
TN de Grooth	run out (Smith)	12	35	26	0	0	46.15
PW Borren*	lbw b Peterson	3	14	13	0	0	23.07
Mudassar Bukhari	b Imran Tahir	0	5	4	0	0	0.00
PM Seelaar	not out	2	15	5	0	0	40.00
BP Loots	lbw b Imran Tahir	6	8	7	0	1	85.71
BA Westdijk	lbw b Imran Tahir	0	2	2	0	0	0.00
Extras	(w 8)	8					
Total	(all out; 34.5 overs; 153 mins)	120	(3.44 runs per over)				

Fall of wickets 1-26 (Kervezee, 5.1 ov), 2-46 (Cooper, 11.5 ov), 3-81 (Zuiderent, 21.3 ov), 4-83 (Barresi, 22.4 ov), 5-100 (ten Doeschate, 27.5 ov), 6-109 (Borren, 31.4 ov), 7-109 (de Grooth, 32.1 ov), 8-110 (Mudassar Bukhari, 32.3 ov), 9-120 (Loots, 34.3 ov), 10-120 (Westdijk, 34.5 ov)

Bowling	O	M	R	W	Econ	
DW Steyn	6	1	26	1	4.33	(3w)
M Morkel	5	0	18	0	3.60	(1w)
JH Kallis	6	0	19	2	3.16	
Imran Tahir	6.5	0	19	3	2.78	(2w)
RJ Peterson	5	0	22	2	4.40	(1w)
JP Duminy	6	0	16	1	2.66	(1w)

South Africa won by 231 runs
Man of the match AB de Villiers (South Africa)

Canada vs. Pakistan

3 March

R Premadasa Stadium, Colombo

Toss Pakistan chose to bat

Umpires DJ Harper (Australia) and NJ Llong (England)

Pakistan innings		R	M	B	4s	6s	SR
Mohammad Hafeez	lbw b Osinde	11	16	12	2	0	91.66
Ahmed Shehzad	c Gordon b Baidwan	12	48	23	2	0	52.17
Kamran Akmal†	c Kumar b Rizwan Cheema	16	66	38	2	0	42.10
Younis Khan	lbw b Baidwan	6	17	13	1	0	46.15
Misbah-ul-Haq	c †Bagai b Balaji Rao	37	104	68	1	0	54.41
Umar Akmal	lbw b Balaji Rao	48	77	68	4	1	70.58
Shahid Afridi*	c Kumar b Rizwan Cheema	20	21	17	2	0	117.64
Abdul Razzaq	lbw b Hansra	8	12	8	1	0	100.00
Umar Gul	not out	2	12	4	0	0	50.00
Wahab Riaz	c Balaji Rao b Hansra	0	1	3	0	0	0.00
Saeed Ajmal	b Baidwan	0	6	5	0	0	0.00
Extras	(b 4, lb 3, w 16, nb 1)	24					
Total	(all out; 43 overs; 195 mins)	184	(4.27 runs per over)				

Fall of wickets 1-16 (Mohammad Hafeez, 3.1 ov), 2-42 (Ahmed Shehzad, 8.5 ov), 3-55 (Younis Khan, 12.5 ov), 4-67 (Kamran Akmal, 15.3 ov), 5-140 (Umar Akmal, 34.6 ov), 6-165 (Misbah-ul-Haq, 38.2 ov), 7-181 (Shahid Afridi, 40.5 ov), 8-181 (Abdul Razzaq, 41.1 ov), 9-181 (Wahab Riaz, 41.4 ov), 10-184 (Saeed Ajmal, 42.6 ov)

Bowling	O	M	R	W	Econ	
Khurram Chohan	3.3	0	10	0	2.85	(1nb)
H Osinde	7	1	25	1	3.57	(5w)
TG Gordon	0.3	0	1	0	2.00	(1w)
HS Baidwan	8	1	35	3	4.37	(2w)
Rizwan Cheema	8	0	33	2	4.12	(3w)
WD Balaji Rao	10	0	50	2	5.00	(1w)
AS Hansra	6	1	23	2	3.83	

Canada innings		R	M	B	4s	6s	SR
R Gunasekera	lbw b Umar Gul	8	20	16	0	0	50.00
NR Kumar	b Abdul Razzaq	2	25	13	0	0	15.38
ZE Surkari	lbw b Saeed Ajmal	27	117	67	2	0	40.29
A Bagai*†	lbw b Shahid Afridi	16	52	35	2	0	45.71
AS Hansra	b Shahid Afridi	43	70	75	4	1	57.33
Rizwan Cheema	b Shahid Afridi	4	5	8	1	0	50.00
TG Gordon	c Wahab Riaz b Shahid Afridi	9	17	12	1	0	75.00
HS Baidwan	b Shahid Afridi	0	1	1	0	0	0.00
Khurram Chohan	not out	5	31	20	0	0	25.00
WD Balaji Rao	run out (Shahid Afridi)	1	14	7	0	0	14.28
H Osinde	b Wahab Riaz	0	5	3	0	0	0.00
Extras	(lb 4, w 19)	23					
Total	(all out; 42.5 overs; 185 mins)	138	(3.22 runs per over)				

Fall of wickets 1-16 (Gunasekera, 3.6 ov), 2-16 (Kumar, 4.5 ov), 3-44 (Bagai, 17.1 ov), 4-104 (Surkari, 33.3 ov), 5-111 (Rizwan Cheema, 34.6 ov), 6-114 (Hansra, 36.4 ov), 7-114 (Baidwan, 36.5 ov), 8-130 (Gordon, 38.4 ov), 9-134 (Balaji Rao, 41.4 ov), 10-138 (Osinde, 42.5 ov)

Bowling	O	M	R	W	Econ	
Abdul Razzaq	7	2	16	1	2.28	(1w)
Umar Gul	7	1	20	1	2.85	(4w)
Shahid Afridi	10	0	23	5	2.30	(3w)
Wahab Riaz	5.5	0	23	1	3.94	(2w)
Saeed Ajmal	8	0	31	1	3.87	(3w)
Mohammad Hafeez	5	0	21	0	4.20	

Pakistan won by 46 runs

Man of the match Shahid Afridi (Pakistan)

New Zealand vs. Zimbabwe
4 March
Sardar Patel Stadium, Motera, Ahmedabad
Toss Zimbabwe chose to bat
Umpires Aleem Dar (Pakistan) and M Erasmus (South Africa)

Zimbabwe innings		R	M	B	4s	6s	SR
BRM Taylor	lbw b Styris	44	106	57	4	0	77.19
CK Coventry	run out (Bennett)	0	7	2	0	0	0.00
T Taibu†	lbw b Southee	8	28	18	1	0	44.44
CR Ervine	c Ryder b Mills	11	25	25	2	0	44.00
E Chigumbura*	lbw b Vettori	1	9	4	0	0	25.00
RW Chakabva	c Taylor b Vettori	0	3	2	0	0	0.00
GA Lamb	run out (Guptill/Vettori)	18	46	34	1	0	52.94
P Utseya	b Southee	36	95	65	3	0	55.38
AG Cremer	c †BB McCullum b Mills	22	43	43	1	0	51.16
RW Price	lbw b Southee	11	27	19	0	0	57.89
T Panyangara	not out	4	13	9	1	0	44.44
Extras	(lb 4, w 3)	7					
Total	(all out; 46.2 overs; 202 mins)	162	(3.49 runs per over)				

Fall of wickets 1-2 (Coventry, 1.2 ov), 2-27 (Taibu, 7.4 ov), 3-42 (Ervine, 12.6 ov), 4-46 (Chigumbura, 14.1 ov), 5-46 (Chakabva, 14.3 ov), 6-86 (Taylor, 23.1 ov), 7-89 (Lamb, 26.6 ov), 8-122 (Cremer, 36.6 ov), 9-157 (Price, 44.1 ov), 10-162 (Utseya, 46.2 ov)

Bowling	O	M	R	W	Econ	
KD Mills	10	0	29	2	2.90	(1w)
TG Southee	9.2	3	29	3	3.10	(2w)
HK Bennett	8	0	37	0	4.62	
DL Vettori	10	3	25	2	2.50	
SB Styris	4	0	13	1	3.25	
NL McCullum	3	0	15	0	5.00	
JD Ryder	2	0	10	0	5.00	

New Zealand innings		R	M	B	4s	6s	SR
MJ Guptill	not out	86	114	108	7	2	79.62
BB McCullum†	not out	76	114	95	6	2	80.00
Extras	(lb 1, w 1, nb 2)	4					
Total	(0 wickets; 33.3 overs; 114 mins)	166	(4.95 runs per over)				

Did not bat JD Ryder, LRPL Taylor, JEC Franklin, SB Styris, NL McCullum, DL Vettori*, KD Mills, TG Southee, HK Bennett

Bowling	O	M	R	W	Econ	
T Panyangara	5.3	0	42	0	7.63	(1nb)
RW Price	7	0	23	0	3.28	
P Utseya	6	0	23	0	3.83	(1nb)
GA Lamb	5	0	18	0	3.60	
AG Cremer	7	0	38	0	5.42	
E Chigumbura	3	0	21	0	7.00	(1w)

New Zealand won by 10 wickets
Man of the Match MJ Guptill (New Zealand)

Bangladesh vs. West Indies
4 March
Shere Bangla National Stadium, Mirpur
Toss Bangladesh chose to bat
Umpires SJ Davis (Australia) and HDPK Dharmasena (Sri Lanka)

Bangladesh innings		R	M	B	4s	6s	SR
Tamim Iqbal	c Sammy b Roach	0	2	3	0	0	0.00
Imrul Kayes	c †Thomas b Sammy	5	15	8	0	0	62.50
Junaid Siddique	lbw b Roach	25	33	27	4	0	92.59
Mushfiqur Rahim†	c Sarwan b Sammy	0	6	4	0	0	0.00
Shakib Al Hasan*	b Benn	8	23	16	1	0	50.00
Raqibul Hasan	c Pollard b Sammy	4	23	17	0	0	23.52
Mohammad Ashraful	c †Thomas b Roach	11	33	21	2	0	52.38
Naeem Islam	c †Thomas b Benn	1	14	4	0	0	25.00
Shafiul Islam	c Pollard b Benn	0	12	6	0	0	0.00
Abdur Razzak	not out	2	9	6	0	0	33.33
Rubel Hossain	b Benn	0	2	2	0	0	0.00
Extras	(w 1, nb 1)	2					
Total	(all out; 18.5 overs; 90 mins)	58	(3.07 runs per over)				

Fall of wickets 1-0 (Tamim Iqbal, 0.3 ov), 2-16 (Imrul Kayes, 3.3 ov), 3-25 (Mushfiqur Rahim, 5.1 ov), 4-36 (Junaid Siddique, 8.2 ov), 5-41 (Shakib Al Hasan, 10.2 ov), 6-51 (Raqibul Hasan, 13.6 ov), 7-56 (Naeem Islam, 16.2 ov), 8-56 (Mohammad Ashraful, 17.1 ov), 9-58 (Shafiul Islam, 18.3 ov), 10-58 (Rubel Hossain, 18.5 ov)

Bowling	O	M	R	W	Econ	
KAJ Roach	6	0	19	3	3.16	(1nb, 1w)
SJ Benn	5.5	2	18	4	3.08	
DJG Sammy	7	0	21	3	3.00	

West Indies innings		R	M	B	4s	6s	SR
DS Smith	b Naeem Islam	6	23	12	1	0	50.00
CH Gayle	not out	37	44	36	6	0	102.77
DM Bravo	not out	9	20	26	1	0	34.61
Extras	(b 2, w 5)	7					
Total	(1 wicket; 12.2 overs; 44 mins)	59	(4.78 runs per over)				

Did not bat RR Sarwan, S Chanderpaul, KA Pollard, DC Thomas†, DJG Sammy*, NO Miller, SJ Benn, KAJ Roach
Fall of wickets 1-29 (Smith, 5.1 ov)

Bowling	O	M	R	W	Econ	
Shafiul Islam	2	0	11	0	5.50	
Naeem Islam	6	1	14	1	2.33	(1w)
Rubel Hossain	1	0	12	0	12.00	
Abdur Razzak	1	0	8	0	8.00	(2w)
Mohammad Ashraful	2	0	11	0	5.50	
Shakib Al Hasan	0.2	0	1	0	3.00	

West Indies won by 9 wickets
Man of the match KAJ Roach (West Indies)

Sri Lanka vs. Australia

5 March
R Premadasa Stadium, Colombo
Toss Sri Lanka chose to bat
Umpires IJ Gould (England) and AL Hill (New Zealand)

Sri Lanka innings		R	M	B	4s	6s	SR
WU Tharanga	c Smith b Lee	6	32	18	0	0	33.33
TM Dilshan	c White b Tait	4	7	4	1	0	100.00
KC Sangakkara*†	not out	73	147	102	7	0	71.56
DPMD Jayawardene	run out (Smith)	23	47	25	3	0	92.00
TT Samaraweera	not out	34	74	48	2	0	70.83
Extras	(lb 1, w 5)	6					
Total	(3 wickets; 32.5 overs; 155 mins)	146	(4.44 runs per over)				

Did not bat LPC Silva, AD Mathews, HMRKB Herath, SL Malinga, M Muralitharan, BAW Mendis
Fall of wickets 1-6 (Dilshan, 1.4 ov), 2-31 (Tharanga, 6.4 ov), 3-75 (Jayawardene, 15.2 ov)

Bowling	O	M	R	W	Econ	
B Lee	5	0	27	1	5.40	(2w)
SW Tait	5	0	23	1	4.60	
SR Watson	7	0	29	0	4.14	
MG Johnson	4	0	15	0	3.75	(2w)
JJ Krejza	7.5	0	34	0	4.34	(1w)
SPD Smith	4	0	17	0	4.25	

Australia team
SR Watson, BJ Haddin†, RT Ponting*, MJ Clarke, DJ Hussey, CL White, SPD Smith, MG Johnson, JJ Krejza, B Lee, SW Tait

No result

England vs. South Africa
6 March
MA Chidambaram Stadium, Chepauk, Chennai
Toss England chose to bat
Umpires AM Saheba and SJA Taufel (Australia)

England innings		R	M	B	4s	6s	SR
AJ Strauss*	c de Villiers b Peterson	0	1	3	0	0	0.00
KP Pietersen	c Kallis b Peterson	2	5	3	0	0	66.66
IJL Trott	c & b Imran Tahir	52	123	94	3	0	55.31
IR Bell	c & b Peterson	5	14	7	1	0	71.42
RS Bopara	lbw b Morkel	60	149	98	3	1	61.22
MJ Prior†	c †van Wyk b Morkel	10	24	19	1	0	52.63
MH Yardy	c Peterson b Imran Tahir	3	40	17	0	0	17.64
TT Bresnan	lbw b Steyn	1	5	4	0	0	25.00
GP Swann	c Duminy b Imran Tahir	16	28	20	3	0	80.00
SCJ Broad	lbw b Imran Tahir	0	2	3	0	0	0.00
JM Anderson	not out	2	10	6	0	0	33.33
Extras	(b 1, lb 7, w 12)	20					
Total	(all out; 45.4 overs; 205 mins)	171	(3.74 runs per over)				

Fall of wickets 1-1 (Strauss, 0.3 ov), 2-3 (Pietersen, 0.6 ov), 3-15 (Bell, 4.4 ov), 4-114 (Trott, 29.5 ov), 5-134 (Prior, 35.3 ov), 6-148 (Bopara, 39.3 ov), 7-149 (Bresnan, 40.1 ov), 8-161 (Yardy, 43.2 ov), 9-161 (Broad, 43.5 ov), 10-171 (Swann, 45.4 ov)

Bowling	O	M	R	W	Econ	
RJ Peterson	8	2	22	3	2.75	(1w)
DW Steyn	9	0	37	1	4.11	(1w)
M Morkel	7	0	16	2	2.28	(1w)
JH Kallis	4	1	14	0	3.50	(1w)
Imran Tahir	8.4	1	38	4	4.38	(1w)
F du Plessis	5	0	16	0	3.20	
JP Duminy	4	0	20	0	5.00	(1w)

South Africa innings		R	M	B	4s	6s	SR
HM Amla	b Broad	42	81	51	2	0	82.35
GC Smith*	c †Prior b Swann	22	63	41	2	0	53.65
JH Kallis	c †Prior b Broad	15	26	20	3	0	75.00
AB de Villiers	b Anderson	25	56	44	0	0	56.81
F du Plessis	run out (Bell/†Prior)	17	52	38	2	0	44.73
JP Duminy	b Anderson	0	12	4	0	0	0.00
MN van Wyk†	b Bresnan	13	67	37	0	0	35.13
RJ Peterson	c †Prior b Yardy	3	15	16	0	0	18.75
DW Steyn	lbw b Broad	20	51	31	3	0	64.51
M Morkel	c †Prior b Broad	1	10	3	0	0	33.33
Imran Tahir	not out	1	2	1	0	0	100.00
Extras	(lb 2, w 4)	6					
Total	(all out; 47.4 overs; 222 mins)	165	(3.46 runs per over)				

Fall of wickets 1-63 (Smith, 14.1 ov), 2-75 (Amla, 17.3 ov), 3-82 (Kallis, 19.2 ov), 4-124 (de Villiers, 31.6 ov), 5-124 (du Plessis, 32.2 ov), 6-124 (Duminy, 33.4 ov), 7-127 (Peterson, 36.6 ov), 8-160 (van Wyk, 46.2 ov), 9-164 (Steyn, 47.1 ov), 10-165 (Morkel, 47.4 ov)

Bowling	O	M	R	W	Econ	
MH Yardy	9	1	46	1	5.11	
JM Anderson	6	0	16	2	2.66	(3w)
TT Bresnan	8	1	27	1	3.37	
GP Swann	10	2	29	1	2.90	
SCJ Broad	6.4	0	15	4	2.25	
KP Pietersen	8	0	30	0	3.75	

England won by 6 runs
Man of the match RS Bopara (England)

India vs. Ireland
6 March
M Chinnaswamy Stadium, Bangalore
Toss India chose to field
Umpires BF Bowden (New Zealand) and RJ Tucker (Australia)

Ireland innings		R	M	B	4s	6s	SR
WTS Porterfield*	c Harbhajan Singh b Yuvraj Singh	75	146	104	6	1	72.11
PR Stirling	b Khan	0	2	1	0	0	0.00
EC Joyce	c †Dhoni b Khan	4	8	5	1	0	80.00
NJ O'Brien†	run out (Kohli/†Dhoni)	46	93	78	3	0	58.97
AR White	c †Dhoni b Yuvraj Singh	5	8	10	0	0	50.00
KJ O'Brien	c & b Yuvraj Singh	9	14	13	1	0	69.23
AR Cusack	lbw b Yuvraj Singh	24	49	30	3	0	80.00
JF Mooney	lbw b Yuvraj Singh	5	19	17	0	0	29.41
DT Johnston	lbw b Patel	17	38	20	2	0	85.00
GH Dockrell	c †Dhoni b Khan	3	19	10	0	0	30.00
WB Rankin	not out	1	5	1	0	0	100.00
Extras	(lb 4, w 8, nb 6)	18					
Total	(all out; 47.5 overs; 205 mins)	207	(4.32 runs per over)				

Fall of wickets 1-1 (Stirling, 0.4 ov), 2-9 (Joyce, 2.3 ov), 3-122 (NJ O'Brien, 26.5 ov), 4-129 (White, 29.1 ov), 5-147 (KJ O'Brien, 33.4 ov), 6-160 (Porterfield, 37.1 ov), 7-178 (Mooney, 41.5 ov), 8-184 (Cusack, 43.4 ov), 9-201 (Dockrell, 46.6 ov), 10-207 (Johnston, 47.5 ov)

Bowling	O	M	R	W	Econ	
Z Khan	9	1	30	3	3.33	(1w)
MM Patel	4.5	0	25	1	5.17	(1w)
YK Pathan	7	1	32	0	4.57	
Harbhajan Singh	9	1	29	0	3.22	(1w)
PP Chawla	8	0	56	0	7.00	(2nb, 3w)
Yuvraj Singh	10	0	31	5	3.10	(1w)

India innings		R	M	B	4s	6s	SR
V Sehwag	c & b Johnston	5	5	3	1	0	166.66
SR Tendulkar	lbw b Dockrell	38	91	56	4	0	67.85
G Gambhir	c Cusack b Johnston	10	18	15	2	0	66.66
V Kohli	run out (Dockrell/KJ O'Brien)	34	82	53	3	0	64.15
Yuvraj Singh	not out	50	108	75	3	0	66.66
MS Dhoni*†	lbw b Dockrell	34	68	50	2	0	68.00
YK Pathan	not out	30	23	24	2	3	125.00
Extras	(lb 4, w 5)	9					
Total	(5 wickets; 46 overs; 200 mins)	210	(4.56 runs per over)				

Did not bat Harbhajan Singh, PP Chawla, Z Khan, MM Patel
Fall of wickets 1-9 (Sehwag, 1.1 ov), 2-24 (Gambhir, 5.2 ov), 3-87 (Tendulkar, 20.1 ov), 4-100 (Kohli, 23.4 ov), 5-167 (Dhoni, 40.1 ov)

Bowling	O	M	R	W	Econ	
WB Rankin	10	1	34	0	3.40	(2w)
DT Johnston	5	1	16	2	3.20	(1w)
GH Dockrell	10	0	49	2	4.90	
JF Mooney	2	0	18	0	9.00	
PR Stirling	10	0	45	0	4.50	(2w)
AR White	5	0	23	0	4.60	
KJ O'Brien	1	0	3	0	3.00	
AR Cusack	3	0	18	0	6.00	

India won by 5 wickets (with 24 balls remaining)
Man of the match Yuvraj Singh (India)

Canada vs. Kenya

7 March
Feroz Shah Kotla, Delhi
Toss Kenya chose to bat
Umpires **Asad Rauf** (Pakistan) and **BR Doctrove** (West Indies)

Kenya innings		R	M	B	4s	6s	SR
MA Ouma†	c Baidwan b Osinde	0	2	2	0	0	0.00
SR Waters	b Osinde	2	22	13	0	0	15.38
CO Obuya	b Baidwan	31	53	35	3	1	88.57
DO Obuya	c †Bagai b Osinde	2	11	8	0	0	25.00
SO Tikolo	lbw b Rizwan Cheema	12	39	20	1	0	60.00
T Mishra	c Surkari b Davison	51	120	73	3	0	69.86
JK Kamande*	c †Bagai b Balaji Rao	22	49	58	3	0	37.93
TM Odoyo	b Baidwan	51	86	62	5	1	82.25
NN Odhiambo	b Osinde	4	8	9	0	0	44.44
E Otieno	c Hansra b Rizwan Cheema	8	20	17	1	0	47.05
JO Ngoche	not out	1	6	3	0	0	33.33
Extras	(lb 4, w 10)	14					
Total	(all out; 50 overs; 214 mins)	**198**	(3.96 runs per over)				

Fall of wickets 1-0 (Ouma, 0.2 ov), 2-7 (Waters, 4.5 ov), 3-21 (DO Obuya, 6.6 ov), 4-41 (CO Obuya, 11.3 ov), 5-57 (Tikolo, 14.6 ov), 6-109 (Kamande, 29.2 ov), 7-166 (Mishra, 42.1 ov), 8-171 (Odhiambo, 43.6 ov), 9-193 (Otieno, 48.6 ov), 10-198 (Odoyo, 49.6 ov)

Bowling	O	M	R	W	Econ	
H Osinde	10	2	26	4	2.60	(3w)
HS Baidwan	10	1	41	2	4.10	(2w)
PA Desai	3	0	20	0	6.66	
Rizwan Cheema	9	1	30	2	3.33	
AS Hansra	3	0	15	0	5.00	
WD Balaji Rao	10	0	36	1	3.60	(1w)
JM Davison	5	0	26	1	5.20	

Canada innings		R	M	B	4s	6s	SR
R Gunasekera	st †Ouma b Ngoche	18	59	27	3	0	66.66
Rizwan Cheema	b Otieno	17	18	13	2	1	130.76
ZE Surkari	run out (Kamande)	10	29	26	1	0	38.46
A Bagai*†	not out	64	150	97	7	0	65.97
AS Hansra	c Ngoche b Odhiambo	70	121	99	7	2	70.70
TG Gordon	b Odhiambo	3	12	11	0	0	27.27
JM Davison	not out	4	4	1	1	0	400.00
Extras	(b 1, w 11, nb 1)	13					
Total	(5 wickets; 45.3 overs; 199 mins)	**199**	(4.37 runs per over)				

Did not bat HS Baidwan, PA Desai, H Osinde, WD Balaji Rao
Fall of wickets 1-19 (Rizwan Cheema, 3.4 ov), 2-37 (Surkari, 9.5 ov), 3-48 (Gunasekera, 11.0 ov), 4-180 (Hansra, 42.5 ov), 5-186 (Gordon, 44.5 ov)

Bowling	O	M	R	W	Econ	
TM Odoyo	5	1	18	0	3.60	
E Otieno	8.3	0	45	1	5.29	(1nb, 4w)
NN Odhiambo	10	0	45	2	4.50	
JO Ngoche	10	2	26	1	2.60	(1w)
JK Kamande	5	0	25	0	5.00	(1w)
CO Obuya	2	0	15	0	7.50	(1w)
SO Tikolo	5	1	24	0	4.80	

Canada won by 5 wickets (with 27 balls remaining)
Man of the match H Osinde (Canada)

New Zealand vs. Pakistan
8 March
Pallekele International Cricket Stadium
Toss New Zealand chose to bat
Umpires DJ Harper (Australia) and NJ Llong (England)

New Zealand innings		R	M	B	4s	6s	SR
MJ Guptill	b Shahid Afridi	57	123	86	6	0	66.27
BB McCullum†	b Shoaib Akhtar	6	3	3	0	1	200.00
JM How	lbw b Umar Gul	4	50	29	0	0	13.79
LRPL Taylor	not out	131	171	124	8	7	105.64
JEC Franklin	lbw b Mohammad Hafeez	1	5	2	0	0	50.00
SB Styris	lbw b Umar Gul	28	52	37	1	0	75.67
NL McCullum	b Umar Gul	19	16	10	1	2	190.00
JDP Oram	c Umar Gul b Abdur Rehman	25	23	9	1	3	277.77
KD Mills	not out	7	2	3	1	0	233.33
Extras	(lb 10, w 11, nb 3)	24					
Total	(7 wickets; 50 overs; 226 mins)	302	(6.04 runs per over)				

Did not bat DL Vettori*, TG Southee
Fall of wickets 1-8 (BB McCullum, 0.4 ov), 2-55 (How, 12.3 ov), 3-112 (Guptill, 28.5 ov), 4-113 (Franklin, 29.1 ov), 5-175 (Styris, 41.6 ov), 6-210 (NL McCullum, 45.5 ov), 7-295 (Oram, 49.3 ov)

Bowling	O	M	R	W	Econ	
Shoaib Akhtar	9	0	70	1	7.77	(3nb, 3w)
Abdur Rehman	10	0	60	1	6.00	(1w)
Umar Gul	10	1	32	3	3.20	(2w)
Abdul Razzaq	4	0	49	0	12.25	(4w)
Shahid Afridi	10	0	55	1	5.50	
Mohammad Hafeez	7	0	26	1	3.71	(1w)

Pakistan innings		R	M	B	4s	6s	SR
Mohammad Hafeez	lbw b Southee	5	6	6	1	0	83.33
Ahmed Shehzad	lbw b Mills	10	29	16	1	0	62.50
Kamran Akmal†	c Taylor b Southee	8	29	16	1	0	50.00
Younis Khan	b Mills	0	2	3	0	0	0.00
Misbah-ul-Haq	c Styris b Southee	7	36	31	0	0	22.58
Umar Akmal	c Oram b NL McCullum	38	95	58	3	0	65.51
Shahid Afridi*	b Oram	17	13	9	2	1	188.88
Abdul Razzaq	c Oram b Styris	62	108	74	9	0	83.78
Abdur Rehman	lbw b NL McCullum	1	20	10	0	0	10.00
Umar Gul	not out	34	41	25	3	1	136.00
Shoaib Akhtar	c NL McCullum b Styris	0	2	2	0	0	0.00
Extras	(lb 6, w 4)	10					
Total	(all out; 41.4 overs; 195 mins)	192	(4.60 runs per over)				

Fall of wickets 1-5 (Mohammad Hafeez, 1.2 ov), 2-23 (Ahmed Shehzad, 6.1 ov), 3-23 (Younis Khan, 6.4 ov), 4-23 (Kamran Akmal, 7.1 ov), 5-45 (Misbah-ul-Haq, 14.4 ov), 6-66 (Shahid Afridi, 17.1 ov), 7-102 (Umar Akmal, 28.3 ov), 8-125 (Abdur Rehman, 32.4 ov), 9-191 (Abdul Razzaq, 41.1 ov), 10-192 (Shoaib Akhtar, 41.4 ov)

Bowling	O	M	R	W	Econ	
KD Mills	8	1	43	2	5.37	
TG Southee	8	1	25	3	3.12	
JDP Oram	10	1	47	1	4.70	
JEC Franklin	5	0	26	0	5.20	
NL McCullum	6	0	28	2	4.66	(1w)
SB Styris	4.4	0	17	2	3.64	

New Zealand won by 110 runs
Man of the match LRPL Taylor (New Zealand)

India vs. Netherlands
9 March
Feroz Shah Kotla, Delhi
Toss Netherlands chose to bat
Umpires SJ Davis (Australia) and BNJ Oxenford (Australia)

Netherlands innings		R	M	B	4s	6s	SR
ES Szwarczynski	b Chawla	28	59	42	4	0	66.66
W Barresi†	lbw b Yuvraj Singh	26	67	58	2	0	44.82
TLW Cooper	c †Dhoni b Nehra	29	52	47	2	0	61.70
RN ten Doeschate	c Khan b Yuvraj Singh	11	29	28	1	0	39.28
AN Kervezee	c Harbhajan Singh b Chawla	11	45	23	1	0	47.82
B Zuiderent	lbw b Khan	0	10	6	0	0	0.00
TN de Grooth	run out (Chawla/†Dhoni)	5	14	11	0	0	45.45
PW Borren*	c Nehra b Khan	38	46	36	3	2	105.55
BP Kruger	run out (Kohli/†Dhoni)	8	16	12	1	0	66.66
Mudassar Bukhari	b Khan	21	20	18	1	2	116.66
PM Seelaar	not out	0	2	0	0	0	-
Extras	(b 6, lb 3, w 2, nb 1)	12					
Total	(all out; 46.4 overs; 191 mins)	189	(4.05 runs per over)				

Fall of wickets 1-56 (Szwarczynski, 15.2 ov), 2-64 (Barresi, 18.6 ov), 3-99 (ten Doeschate, 28.2 ov), 4-100 (Cooper, 29.1 ov), 5-101 (Zuiderent, 30.6 ov), 6-108 (de Grooth, 34.2 ov), 7-127 (Kervezee, 38.1 ov), 8-151 (Kruger, 42.2 ov), 9-189 (Borren, 46.1 ov), 10-189 (Mudassar Bukhari, 46.4 ov)

Bowling	O	M	R	W	Econ	
Z Khan	6.4	0	20	3	3.00	
A Nehra	5	1	22	1	4.40	
YK Pathan	6	1	17	0	2.83	
Harbhajan Singh	10	0	31	0	3.10	(2w)
PP Chawla	10	0	47	2	4.70	(1nb)
Yuvraj Singh	9	1	43	2	4.77	

India innings		R	M	B	4s	6s	SR
V Sehwag	c Kervezee b Seelaar	39	36	26	5	2	150.00
SR Tendulkar	c Kruger b Seelaar	27	45	22	6	0	122.72
YK Pathan	c & b Seelaar	11	12	10	1	1	110.00
G Gambhir	b Mudassar Bukhari	28	57	28	3	0	100.00
V Kohli	b Borren	12	16	20	2	0	60.00
Yuvraj Singh	not out	51	93	73	7	0	69.86
MS Dhoni*†	not out	19	56	40	2	0	47.50
Extras	(w 4)	4					
Total	(5 wickets; 36.3 overs; 160 mins)	191	(5.23 runs per over)				

Did not bat Harbhajan Singh, PP Chawla, Z Khan, A Nehra
Fall of wickets 1-69 (Sehwag, 7.3 ov), 2-80 (Tendulkar, 9.1 ov), 3-82 (Pathan, 9.5 ov), 4-99 (Kohli, 14.3 ov), 5-139 (Gambhir, 23.1 ov)

Bowling	O	M	R	W	Econ	
Mudassar Bukhari	6	1	33	1	5.50	(2w)
RN ten Doeschate	7	0	38	0	5.42	(2w)
PM Seelaar	10	1	53	3	5.30	
PW Borren	8	0	33	1	4.12	
TLW Cooper	2	0	11	0	5.50	
BP Kruger	3.3	0	23	0	6.57	

India won by 5 wickets (with 81 balls remaining)
Man of the match Yuvraj Singh (India)

Sri Lanka vs. Zimbabwe
10 March
Pallekele International Cricket Stadium
Toss Zimbabwe chose to field
Umpires M Erasmus (South Africa) and NJ Llong (England)

Sri Lanka innings		R	M	B	4s	6s	SR
WU Tharanga	c Chigumbura b Mpofu	133	182	141	17	0	94.32
TM Dilshan	c Panyangara b Utseya	144	186	131	16	1	109.92
NLTC Perera	c Chigumbura b Price	3	5	5	0	0	60.00
DPMD Jayawardene	c Chakabva b Mpofu	9	7	7	1	0	128.57
KC Sangakkara*†	not out	11	7	7	1	0	157.14
AD Mathews	c Chigumbura b Mpofu	0	1	1	0	0	0.00
LPC Silva	c Panyangara b Mpofu	4	2	2	1	0	200.00
TT Samaraweera	not out	8	7	7	1	0	114.28
Extras	(b 2, lb 3, w 9, nb 1)	15					
Total	(6 wickets; 50 overs)	327	(6.54 runs per over)				

Did not bat KMDN Kulasekara, SL Malinga, M Muralitharan
Fall of wickets 1-282 (Tharanga, 44.4 ov), 2-289 (Dilshan, 45.4 ov), 3-296 (Perera, 46.3 ov), 4-300 (Jayawardene, 47.1 ov), 5-302 (Mathews, 47.3 ov), 6-308 (Silva, 47.6 ov)

Bowling	O	M	R	W	Econ	
CB Mpofu	7	0	62	4	8.85	(1nb, 2w)
T Panyangara	6	0	51	0	8.50	(2w)
RW Price	9	1	46	1	5.11	(2w)
E Chigumbura	3	0	20	0	6.66	
P Utseya	10	0	50	1	5.00	(1w)
Cremer	7	0	42	0	6.00	(1w)
GA Lamb	8	0	51	0	6.37	(1w)

Zimbabwe innings		R	M	B	4s	6s	SR
BRM Taylor	c Jayawardene b Mathews	80	101	72	9	1	111.11
RW Chakabva	b Muralitharan	35	83	61	3	0	57.37
T Taibu†	c †Sangakkara b Mathews	4	8	6	0	0	66.66
P Utseya	st †Sangakkara b Dilshan	4	21	11	0	0	36.36
CR Ervine	lbw b Dilshan	17	23	21	2	0	80.95
E Chigumbura*	c Perera b Muralitharan	6	21	11	0	0	54.54
GA Lamb	c Jayawardene b Dilshan	0	1	1	0	0	0.00
AG Cremer	not out	14	42	27	1	0	51.85
RW Price	c Samaraweera b Perera	11	22	15	2	0	73.33
T Panyangara	lbw b Dilshan	0	2	4	0	0	0.00
CB Mpofu	b Muralitharan	1	4	5	0	0	20.00
Extras	(b 2, lb 2, w 12)	16					
Total	(all out; 39 overs)	188	(4.82 runs per over)				

Fall of wickets 1-116 (Chakabva, 19.5 ov), 2-125 (Taibu, 22.1 ov), 3-132 (Taylor, 24.1 ov), 4-150 (Utseya, 27.3 ov), 5-156 (Ervine, 29.3 ov), 6-156 (Lamb, 29.4 ov), 7-165 (Chigumbura, 31.5 ov), 8-185 (Price, 36.5 ov), 9-185 (Panyangara, 37.4 ov), 10-188 (Mpofu, 38.6 ov)

Bowling	O	M	R	W	Econ	
SL Malinga	8	0	51	0	6.37	(7w)
KMDN Kulasekara	8	0	33	0	4.12	(1w)
NLTC Perera	6	0	33	1	5.50	
M Muralitharan	9	0	34	3	3.77	
AD Mathews	5	0	29	2	5.80	
TM Dilshan	3	1	4	4	1.33	

Sri Lanka won by 139 runs
Man of the match TM Dilshan (Sri Lanka)

Ireland vs. West Indies
11 March
Punjab Cricket Association Stadium, Mohali, Chandigarh
Toss Ireland chose to field
Umpires EAR de Silva (Sri Lanka) and SK Tarapore

West Indies innings		R	M	B	4s	6s	SR
DS Smith	b KJ O'Brien	107	194	133	11	1	80.45
S Chanderpaul	c Porterfield b KJ O'Brien	35	102	62	3	0	56.45
DM Bravo	b KJ O'Brien	0	2	3	0	0	0.00
RR Sarwan	c Mooney b Dockrell	10	29	19	1	0	52.63
KA Pollard	c Rankin b Mooney	94	83	55	8	5	170.90
DJG Sammy*	c Dockrell b KJ O'Brien	4	1	3	1	0	133.33
DC Thomas†	c †NJ O'Brien b Rankin	2	8	8	0	0	25.00
AD Russell	b Mooney	3	15	7	0	0	42.85
NO Miller	not out	5	9	6	0	0	83.33
SJ Benn	run out (Botha/Mooney)	2	4	2	0	0	100.00
KAJ Roach	c Stirling b Botha	1	1	2	0	0	50.00
Extras	(b 3, lb 6, w 3)	12					
Total	(all out; 50 overs; 232 mins)	275	(5.50 runs per over)				

Fall of wickets 1-89 (Chanderpaul, 24.2 ov), 2-89 (Bravo, 24.5 ov), 3-130 (Sarwan, 31.6 ov), 4-218 (Smith, 42.3 ov), 5-222 (Sammy, 42.6 ov), 6-228 (Thomas, 44.6 ov), 7-267 (Pollard, 48.1 ov), 8-267 (Russell, 48.2 ov), 9-272 (Benn, 49.2 ov), 10-275 (Roach, 49.6 ov)

Bowling	O	M	R	W	Econ	
WB Rankin	10	1	35	1	3.50	
AR Cusack	7	1	22	0	3.14	
JF Mooney	9	0	58	2	6.44	(2w)
AC Botha	10	0	56	1	5.60	
KJ O'Brien	9	0	71	4	7.88	
PR Stirling	2	0	9	0	4.50	
GH Dockrell	3	0	15	1	5.00	(1w)

Ireland innings		R	M	B	4s	6s	SR
WTS Porterfield*	c sub (R Rampaul) b Sammy	11	52	34	2	0	32.35
PR Stirling	c Sammy b Benn	5	7	6	1	0	83.33
EC Joyce	b Russell	84	150	106	9	0	79.24
NJ O'Brien†	b Benn	25	38	31	2	0	80.64
GC Wilson	lbw b Sammy	61	90	62	6	1	98.38
KJ O'Brien	c Pollard b Sammy	5	10	9	0	0	55.55
AR Cusack	st †Thomas b Benn	2	15	5	0	0	40.00
JF Mooney	b Roach	6	18	7	1	0	85.71
AC Botha	run out (Sammy)	0	3	7	0	0	0.00
GH Dockrell	b Benn	19	22	19	3	0	100.00
WB Rankin	not out	5	11	9	0	0	55.55
Extras	(lb 4, w 3, nb 1)	8					
Total	(all out; 49 overs; 217 mins)	231	(4.71 runs per over)				

Fall of wickets 1-6 (Stirling, 1.4 ov), 2-42 (Porterfield, 11.6 ov), 3-86 (NJ O'Brien, 20.6 ov), 4-177 (Joyce, 37.3 ov), 5-187 (KJ O'Brien, 39.4 ov), 6-199 (Wilson, 41.4 ov), 7-199 (Cusack, 42.2 ov), 8-201 (Botha, 43.4 ov), 9-215 (Mooney, 45.5 ov), 10-231 (Dockrell, 48.6 ov)

Bowling	O	M	R	W	Econ	
KAJ Roach	8	0	34	1	4.25	
SJ Benn	10	0	53	4	5.30	(2w)
DJG Sammy	10	3	31	3	3.10	
AD Russell	10	2	37	1	3.70	(1nb)
KA Pollard	5	0	32	0	6.40	(1w)
NO Miller	6	0	40	0	6.66	

West Indies won by 44 runs
Man of the match KA Pollard (West Indies)

Bangladesh vs. England
11 March
Zahur Ahmed Chowdhury Stadium, Chittagong
Toss Bangladesh chose to field
Umpires DJ Harper (Australia) and RJ Tucker (Australia)

England innings		R	M	B	4s	6s	SR
AJ Strauss*	c Junaid Siddique b Naeem Islam	18	48	31	2	0	58.06
MJ Prior†	st †Mushfiqur Rahim b Abdur Razzak	15	35	20	2	0	75.00
IJL Trott	c Junaid Siddique b Shakib Al Hasan	67	138	99	2	0	67.67
IR Bell	c Naeem Islam b Mahmudullah	5	19	23	0	0	21.73
EJG Morgan	c Imrul Kayes b Naeem Islam	63	84	72	8	0	87.50
RS Bopara	c Naeem Islam b Abdur Razzak	16	22	22	1	0	72.72
GP Swann	c & b Shakib Al Hasan	12	12	8	2	0	150.00
PD Collingwood	run out (Mahmudullah)	14	29	13	0	0	107.69
TT Bresnan	c Shafiul Islam b Rubel Hossain	2	2	2	0	0	100.00
A Shahzad	b Shafiul Islam	1	2	3	0	0	33.33
JM Anderson	not out	2	9	5	0	0	40.00
Extras	(lb 2, w 8)	10					
Total	(all out; 49.4 overs; 205 mins)	225	(4.53 runs per over)				

Fall of wickets 1-32 (Prior, 7.0 ov), 2-39 (Strauss, 10.3 ov), 3-53 (Bell, 16.4 ov), 4-162 (Morgan, 38.4 ov), 5-182 (Trott, 43.4 ov), 6-195 (Bopara, 44.5 ov), 7-209 (Swann, 46.4 ov), 8-215 (Bresnan, 47.3 ov), 9-217 (Shahzad, 48.1 ov), 10-225 (Collingwood, 49.4 ov)

Bowling	O	M	R	W	Econ	
Shafiul Islam	8	0	43	1	5.37	(2w)
Rubel Hossain	8.4	0	40	1	4.61	(1w)
Naeem Islam	8	0	29	2	3.62	
Abdur Razzak	10	2	32	2	3.20	(3w)
Mahmudullah	5	0	30	1	6.00	
Shakib Al Hasan	10	0	49	2	4.90	

Bangladesh innings		R	M	B	4s	6s	SR
Tamim Iqbal	b Bresnan	38	36	26	5	0	146.15
Imrul Kayes	run out (†Prior/Shahzad)	60	151	100	5	0	60.00
Junaid Siddique	run out (Anderson)	12	17	12	2	0	100.00
Raqibul Hasan	b Shahzad	0	6	2	0	0	0.00
Shakib Al Hasan*	b Swann	32	108	58	1	0	55.17
Mushfiqur Rahim†	c †Prior b Shahzad	6	24	20	1	0	30.00
Mahmudullah	not out	21	61	42	2	0	50.00
Naeem Islam	b Shahzad	0	6	5	0	0	0.00
Abdur Razzak	c Bresnan b Swann	1	5	5	0	0	20.00
Shafiul Islam	not out	24	43	24	4	1	100.00
Extras	(b 1, lb 9, w 23)	33					
Total	(8 wickets; 49 overs; 235 mins)	227	(4.63 runs per over)				

Did not bat Rubel Hossain
Fall of wickets 1-52 (Tamim Iqbal, 8.4 ov), 2-70 (Junaid Siddique, 12.2 ov), 3-73 (Raqibul Hasan, 13.4 ov), 4-155 (Imrul Kayes, 30.6 ov), 5-162 (Shakib Al Hasan, 35.6 ov), 6-166 (Mushfiqur Rahim, 36.2 ov), 7-166 (Naeem Islam, 38.1 ov), 8-169 (Abdur Razzak, 39.4 ov)

Bowling	O	M	R	W	Econ	
JM Anderson	9	0	54	0	6.00	(3w)
A Shahzad	10	0	43	3	4.30	(5w)
TT Bresnan	10	1	35	1	3.50	(1w)
GP Swann	10	1	42	2	4.20	(2w)
RS Bopara	3	0	19	0	6.33	(3w)
PD Collingwood	7	0	24	0	3.42	

Bangladesh won by 2 wickets (with 6 balls remaining)
Man of the match Imrul Kayes (Bangladesh)

India vs. South Africa
12 March
Vidarbha Cricket Association Stadium, Jamtha, Nagpur
Toss India chose to bat
Umpires IJ Gould (England) and SJA Taufel (Australia)

India innings		R	M	B	4s	6s	SR
V Sehwag	b du Plessis	73	87	66	12	0	110.60
SR Tendulkar	c Duminy b Morkel	111	184	101	8	3	109.90
G Gambhir	c Kallis b Steyn	69	98	75	7	0	92.00
YK Pathan	c Smith b Steyn	0	4	2	0	0	0.00
Yuvraj Singh	c Botha b Kallis	12	15	9	0	1	133.33
MS Dhoni*†	not out	12	37	21	0	0	57.14
V Kohli	c & b Peterson	1	2	3	0	0	33.33
Harbhajan Singh	b Steyn	3	8	9	0	0	33.33
Z Khan	c Morkel b Peterson	0	3	3	0	0	0.00
A Nehra	c Smith b Steyn	0	2	3	0	0	0.00
MM Patel	b Steyn	0	1	1	0	0	0.00
Extras	(lb 2, w 12, nb 1)	15					
Total	(all out; 48.4 overs; 229 mins)	296	(6.08 runs per over)				

Fall of wickets 1-142 (Sehwag, 17.4 ov), 2-267 (Tendulkar, 39.4 ov), 3-268 (Gambhir, 40.1 ov), 4-268 (Pathan, 40.3 ov), 5-283 (Yuvraj Singh, 42.6 ov), 6-286 (Kohli, 43.6 ov), 7-293 (Harbhajan Singh, 46.5 ov), 8-294 (Khan, 47.4 ov), 9-296 (Nehra, 48.3 ov), 10-296 (Patel, 48.4 ov)

Bowling	O	M	R	W	Econ	
DW Steyn	9.4	0	50	5	5.17	(2w)
M Morkel	7	0	59	1	8.42	(1nb)
JH Kallis	8	0	43	1	5.37	(1w)
RJ Peterson	9	0	52	2	5.77	(2w)
JP Duminy	3	0	29	0	9.66	
J Botha	9	0	39	0	4.33	(2w)
F du Plessis	3	0	22	1	7.33	(1w)

South Africa innings		R	M	B	4s	6s	SR
HM Amla	c †Dhoni b Harbhajan Singh	61	114	72	5	0	84.72
GC Smith*	c Tendulkar b Khan	16	39	29	2	0	55.17
JH Kallis	run out (†Dhoni/Harbhajan Singh)	69	120	88	4	0	78.40
AB de Villiers	c Kohli b Harbhajan Singh	52	67	39	6	1	133.33
JP Duminy	st †Dhoni b Harbhajan Singh	23	40	20	2	1	115.00
F du Plessis	not out	25	52	23	0	1	108.69
MN van Wyk†	lbw b Patel	5	7	5	1	0	100.00
J Botha	c sub (SK Raina) b Patel	23	15	15	2	1	153.33
RJ Peterson	not out	18	15	7	2	1	257.14
Extras	(lb 7, w 1)	8					
Total	(7 wickets; 49.4 overs; 236 mins)	300	(6.04 runs per over)				

Did not bat M Morkel, DW Steyn
Fall of wickets 1-41 (Smith, 8.3 ov), 2-127 (Amla, 27.2 ov), 3-173 (Kallis, 35.4 ov), 4-223 (de Villiers, 40.3 ov), 5-238 (Duminy, 42.3 ov), 6-247 (van Wyk, 43.6 ov), 7-279 (Botha, 47.5 ov)

Bowling	O	M	R	W	Econ	
Z Khan	10	0	43	1	4.30	
A Nehra	8.4	0	65	0	7.50	
MM Patel	10	0	65	2	6.50	
YK Pathan	4	0	20	0	5.00	
Yuvraj Singh	8	0	47	0	5.87	
Harbhajan Singh	9	0	53	3	5.88	(1w)

South Africa won by 3 wickets (with 2 balls remaining)
Man of the match DW Steyn (South Africa)

Canada vs. New Zealand
13 March
Wankhede Stadium, Mumbai
Toss Canada chose to field
Umpires BNJ Oxenford (Australia) and SK Tarapore

New Zealand innings		R	M	B	4s	6s	SR
MJ Guptill	c †Bagai b Baidwan	17	45	29	3	0	58.62
BB McCullum†	c Gunasekera b Baidwan	101	163	109	12	2	92.66
JD Ryder	c Osinde b Davison	38	80	56	3	0	67.85
LRPL Taylor*	c Hansra b Balaji Rao	74	60	44	6	5	168.18
NL McCullum	c & b Balaji Rao	10	30	9	2	0	111.11
KS Williamson	not out	34	38	27	4	0	125.92
SB Styris	c Davison b Baidwan	35	21	20	3	2	175.00
JEC Franklin	not out	31	12	8	2	3	387.50
Extras	(b 2, lb 3, w 11, nb 2)	18					
Total	(6 wickets; 50 overs; 226 mins)	358	(7.16 runs per over)				

Did not bat JDP Oram, KD Mills, TG Southee
Fall of wickets 1-53 (Guptill, 9.5 ov), 2-149 (Ryder, 29.2 ov), 3-185 (BB McCullum, 36.4 ov), 4-254 (Taylor, 40.5 ov), 5-259 (NL McCullum, 42.1 ov), 6-318 (Styris, 47.6 ov)

Bowling	O	M	R	W	Econ	
Khurram Chohan	7	0	40	0	5.71	(3w)
H Osinde	7	0	52	0	7.42	(2w)
HS Baidwan	9.1	0	84	3	9.16	(1w)
Rizwan Cheema	4.5	0	64	0	13.24	(2nb)
WD Balaji Rao	10	0	62	2	6.20	(1w)
JM Davison	10	1	30	1	3.00	
AS Hansra	2	0	21	0	10.50	

Canada innings		R	M	B	4s	6s	SR
R Gunasekera	c Taylor b Mills	2	9	7	0	0	28.57
H Patel	c †BB McCullum b Oram	31	61	35	5	1	88.57
ZE Surkari	c Taylor b Mills	1	10	11	0	0	9.09
A Bagai*†	c †BB McCullum b NL McCullum	84	145	87	10	0	96.55
AS Hansra	not out	70	140	105	4	1	66.66
Rizwan Cheema	c †BB McCullum b Oram	2	5	4	0	0	50.00
JM Davison	run out (†BB McCullum)	15	37	21	2	0	71.42
WD Balaji Rao	c NL McCullum b Oram	9	13	9	1	0	100.00
HS Baidwan	c Franklin b Southee	8	14	6	1	0	133.33
Khurram Chohan	c Taylor b Ryder	22	23	16	2	1	137.50
H Osinde	not out	0	1	0	0	0	-
Extras	(b 5, lb 2, w 9, nb 1)	17					
Total	(9 wickets; 50 overs; 237 mins)	261	(5.22 runs per over)				

Fall of wickets 1-2 (Gunasekera, 2.1 ov), 2-4 (Surkari, 4.3 ov), 3-50 (Patel, 12.3 ov), 4-175 (Bagai, 36.6 ov), 5-179 (Rizwan Cheema, 38.1 ov), 5-185* (Hansra, retired not out, 40.1 ov), 6-205 (Balaji Rao, 42.5 ov), 7-213 (Davison, 44.1 ov), 8-222 (Baidwan, 45.2 ov), 9-261 (Khurram Chohan, 49.4 ov)

Bowling	O	M	R	W	Econ	
KD Mills	2.4	1	2	2	0.75	
TG Southee	10	1	36	1	3.60	(1w)
JD Ryder	1.2	0	15	1	11.25	(1w)
JDP Oram	10	1	47	3	4.70	(1w)
JEC Franklin	4	0	31	0	7.75	(1nb)
NL McCullum	8	0	56	1	7.00	
SB Styris	10	0	41	0	4.10	(1w)
KS Williamson	4	0	26	0	6.50	(1w)

New Zealand won by 97 runs
Man of the match BB McCullum (New Zealand)

Australia vs. Kenya
13 March
M Chinnaswamy Stadium, Bangalore
Toss Australia chose to bat
Umpires Asad Rauf (Pakistan) and RA Kettleborough (England)

Australia innings		R	M	B	4s	6s	SR
SR Watson	c †Ouma b Odhiambo	21	32	17	3	1	123.52
BJ Haddin†	c Patel b Kamande	65	109	79	9	1	82.27
RT Ponting*	lbw b CO Obuya	36	83	54	5	0	66.66
MJ Clarke	c Patel b Odhiambo	93	109	80	7	1	116.25
CL White	b Kamande	2	6	6	0	0	33.33
MEK Hussey	c DO Obuya b Odhiambo	54	72	43	4	0	125.58
SPD Smith	not out	17	32	15	2	0	113.33
MG Johnson	not out	12	9	7	2	0	171.42
Extras	(b 2, lb 5, w 16, nb 1)	24					
Total	(6 wickets; 50 overs; 229 mins)	324	(6.48 runs per over)				

Did not bat B Lee, JJ Krejza, SW Tait
Fall of wickets 1-38 (Watson, 7.2 ov), 2-127 (Haddin, 24.4 ov), 3-131 (Ponting, 25.4 ov), 4-143 (White, 26.6 ov), 5-257 (Hussey, 43.1 ov), 6-304 (Clarke, 48.1 ov)

Bowling	O	M	R	W	Econ	
TM Odoyo	10	0	50	0	5.00	(1w)
E Otieno	8	0	75	0	9.37	
NN Odhiambo	10	1	57	3	5.70	(2w)
JO Ngoche	8	0	56	0	7.00	(1w)
JK Kamande	10	0	46	2	4.60	(2w)
CO Obuya	4	0	33	1	8.25	(1nb, 1w)

Kenya innings		R	M	B	4s	6s	SR
MA Ouma†	c †Haddin b Lee	4	14	13	0	0	30.76
AA Obanda	b Tait	14	20	10	0	2	140.00
CO Obuya	not out	98	199	129	9	3	75.96
DO Obuya	run out (Hussey/†Haddin)	12	27	16	2	0	75.00
T Mishra	run out (Clarke)	72	92	89	8	1	80.89
TM Odoyo	b Tait	35	59	38	4	1	92.10
RR Patel	run out (Krejza/Tait)	6	10	7	1	0	85.71
JK Kamande*	not out	0	1	0	0	0	-
Extras	(b 2, lb 6, w 12, nb 3)	23					
Total	(6 wickets; 50 overs; 214 mins)	264	(5.28 runs per over)				

Did not bat NN Odhiambo, E Otieno, JO Ngoche
Fall of wickets 1-12 (Ouma, 2.5 ov), 2-21 (Obanda, 3.6 ov), 3-46 (DO Obuya, 9.4 ov), 4-161 (Mishra, 35.3 ov), 5-247 (Odoyo, 47.3 ov), 6-263 (Patel, 49.4 ov)

Bowling	O	M	R	W	Econ	
B Lee	8	1	26	1	3.25	
SW Tait	8	0	49	2	6.12	(2nb, 5w)
MG Johnson	8	1	40	0	5.00	(2w)
SPD Smith	6	0	36	0	6.00	
JJ Krejza	8	0	36	0	4.50	
MJ Clarke	5	0	21	0	4.20	
SR Watson	7	0	48	0	6.85	(1w)

Australia won by 60 runs
Man of the match CO Obuya (Kenya)

England vs. Netherlands
14 March
Zahur Ahmed Chowdhury Stadium, Chittagong
Toss Netherlands chose to bat
Umpires Aleem Dar (Pakistan) and RJ Tucker (Australia)

Netherlands innings		R	M	B	4s	6s	SR
ES Szwarczynski	run out (Shakib Al Hasan)	28	87	63	0	1	44.44
W Barresi†	lbw b Shakib Al Hasan	10	30	29	1	0	34.48
Mudassar Bukhari	c †Mushfiqur Rahim b Abdur Razzak	6	13	13	1	0	46.15
TLW Cooper	run out (†Mushfiqur Rahim/Shakib Al Hasan)	29	48	41	2	0	70.73
RN ten Doeschate	not out	53	103	71	2	1	74.64
AN Kervezee	st †Mushfiqur Rahim b Suhrawadi Shuvo	18	29	24	2	0	75.00
TN de Grooth	lbw b Abdur Razzak	4	16	15	0	0	26.66
AF Buurman	c Imrul Kayes b Abdur Razzak	0	1	2	0	0	0.00
PW Borren*	run out (†Mushfiqur Rahim/Suhrawadi Shuvo)	3	11	9	0	0	33.33
PM Seelaar	lbw b Rubel Hossain	0	8	6	0	0	0.00
Adeel Raja	run out (Shafiul Islam/Shahriar Nafees)	0	17	5	0	0	0.00
Extras	(lb 9)	9					
Total	(all out; 46.2 overs)	160	(3.45 runs per over)				

Fall of wickets 1-28 (Barresi, 9.1 ov), 2-37 (Mudassar Bukhari, 12.2 ov), 3-66 (Szwarczynski, 22.5 ov), 4-79 (Cooper, 25.1 ov), 5-113 (Kervezee, 33.3 ov), 6-127 (de Grooth, 37.1 ov), 7-127 (Buurman, 37.3 ov), 8-139 (Borren, 40.3 ov), 9-141 (Seelaar, 42.6 ov), 10-160 (Adeel Raja, 46.2 ov)

Bowling	O	M	R	W	Econ
Shafiul Islam	9.2	3	15	0	1.60
Abdur Razzak	10	2	29	3	2.90
Shakib Al Hasan	8	0	38	1	4.75
Rubel Hossain	9	0	36	1	4.00
Suhrawadi Shuvo	10	1	33	1	3.30

Bangladesh innings		R	M	B	4s	6s	SR
Tamim Iqbal	b Mudassar Bukhari	0	1	4	0	0	0.00
Imrul Kayes	not out	73	167	113	6	0	64.60
Junaid Siddique	c Seelaar b Borren	35	91	53	4	0	66.03
Shahriar Nafees	b Cooper	37	56	60	4	0	61.66
Shakib Al Hasan*	c ten Doeschate b Cooper	1	5	7	0	0	14.28
Mushfiqur Rahim†	not out	11	10	12	1	1	91.66
Extras	(b 2, lb 3, w 3, nb 1)	9					
Total	(4 wickets; 41.2 overs; 167 mins)	166	(4.01 runs per over)				

Did not bat Mahmudullah, Suhrawadi Shuvo, Abdur Razzak, Shafiul Islam, Rubel Hossain
Fall of wickets 1-0 (Tamim Iqbal, 0.4 ov), 2-92 (Junaid Siddique, 20.5 ov), 3-151 (Shahriar Nafees, 35.5 ov), 4-153 (Shakib Al Hasan, 37.4 ov)

Bowling	O	M	R	W	Econ	
Mudassar Bukhari	6	2	14	1	2.33	
Adeel Raja	7	0	31	0	4.42	
RN ten Doeschate	6	1	30	0	5.00	(1nb, 3w)
PM Seelaar	10	1	25	0	2.50	
PW Borren	5	0	28	1	5.60	
TLW Cooper	7.2	2	33	2	4.50	

Bangladesh won by 6 wickets (with 52 balls remaining)
Man of the match Imrul Kayes (Bangladesh)

Pakistan vs. Zimbabwe

14 March
Pallekele International Cricket Stadium
Toss Zimbabwe chose to bat
Umpires AL Hill (New Zealand) and NJ Llong (England)

Zimbabwe innings (39.4 overs maximum)		R	M	B	4s	6s	SR
BRM Taylor	c †Kamran Akmal b Abdul Razzaq	4	3	5	1	0	80.00
RW Chakabva	lbw b Umar Gul	0	9	6	0	0	0.00
T Taibu†	c Shahid Afridi b Wahab Riaz	19	54	29	2	0	65.51
V Sibanda	c Misbah-ul-Haq b Umar Gul	5	14	11	1	0	45.45
CR Ervine	b Mohammad Hafeez	52	98	82	5	0	63.41
GA Lamb	c & b Shahid Afridi	16	44	28	1	0	57.14
E Chigumbura*	not out	32	57	46	2	0	69.56
P Utseya	c †Kamran Akmal b Umar Gul	18	36	32	0	0	56.25
AG Cremer	not out	0	0	0	0	0	-
Extras	(lb 2, w 2, nb 1)	5					
Total	(7 wickets; 39.4 overs; 161 mins)	151	(3.80 runs per over)				

Did not bat SW Masakadza, RW Price
Fall of wickets 1-5 (Taylor, 0.5 ov), 2-5 (Chakabva, 1.6 ov), 3-13 (Sibanda, 5.2 ov), 4-43 (Taibu, 12.4 ov), 5-84 (Lamb, 23.5 ov), 6-103 (Ervine, 29.3 ov), 7-151 (Utseya, 39.4 ov)

Bowling	O	M	R	W	Econ	
Abdul Razzaq	7	1	24	1	3.42	(1w)
Umar Gul	7.4	1	36	3	4.69	(1nb)
Wahab Riaz	6	0	21	1	3.50	
Shahid Afridi	8	0	33	1	4.12	
Abdur Rehman	8	1	24	0	3.00	(1w)
Mohammad Hafeez	3	0	11	1	3.66	

Pakistan innings		R	M	B	4s	6s	SR
Mohammad Hafeez	c Price b Utseya	49	97	65	6	0	75.38
Ahmed Shehzad	st †Taibu b Price	8	18	11	2	0	72.72
Asad Shafiq	not out	78	136	97	7	0	80.41
Shahid Afridi*	b Price	3	6	4	0	0	75.00
Younis Khan	not out	13	50	28	0	0	46.42
Extras	(w 13)	13					
Total	(3 wickets; 34.1 overs; 165 mins)	164	(4.80 runs per over)				

Did not bat Misbah-ul-Haq, Abdul Razzaq, Kamran Akmal†, Abdur Rehman, Umar Gul, Wahab Riaz
Fall of wickets 1-17 (Ahmed Shehzad, 3.4 ov), 2-99 (Mohammad Hafeez, 22.2 ov), 3-110 (Shahid Afridi, 23.3 ov)

Bowling	O	M	R	W	Econ	
SW Masakadza	6	1	44	0	7.33	(5w)
RW Price	8	1	21	2	2.62	(3w)
P Utseya	7	1	24	1	3.42	
GA Lamb	7	0	44	0	6.28	
AG Cremer	6.1	0	31	0	5.02	(1w)

Pakistan won by 7 wickets (with 23 balls remaining) (D/L method)
Man of the match Umar Gul (Pakistan)

Ireland vs. South Africa
15 March
Eden Gardens, Kolkata
Toss Ireland chose to field
Umpires HDPK Dharmasena (Sri Lanka) and BR Doctrove (West Indies)

South Africa innings		R	M	B	4s	6s	SR
HM Amla	c Dockrell b Rankin	18	20	17	1	1	105.88
GC Smith*	run out (Mooney)	7	43	18	0	0	38.88
MN van Wyk†	b Dockrell	42	48	41	7	1	102.43
JH Kallis	run out (†NJ O'Brien/Porterfield)	19	43	31	3	0	61.29
JP Duminy	c KJ O'Brien b Mooney	99	139	103	6	1	96.11
F du Plessis	c Johnston b Stirling	11	21	19	0	0	57.89
CA Ingram	b Johnston	46	55	43	7	0	106.97
J Botha	not out	21	47	28	1	0	75.00
RJ Peterson	not out	0	1	0	0	0	-
Extras	(b 2, lb 3, w 4)	9					
Total	(7 wickets; 50 overs; 213 mins)	272	(5.44 runs per over)				

Did not bat M Morkel, DW Steyn
Fall of wickets 1-24 (Amla, 4.4 ov), 2-52 (Smith, 9.4 ov), 3-84 (van Wyk, 15.5 ov), 4-95 (Kallis, 20.3 ov), 5-117 (du Plessis, 26.3 ov), 6-204 (Ingram, 39.4 ov), 7-269 (Duminy, 49.4 ov)

Bowling	O	M	R	W	Econ	
WB Rankin	10	0	59	1	5.90	(1w)
DT Johnston	10	0	76	1	7.60	(1w)
JF Mooney	8	0	36	1	4.50	
GH Dockrell	10	0	37	1	3.70	
PR Stirling	10	0	45	1	4.50	(1w)
AR Cusack	2	0	14	0	7.00	(1w)

Ireland innings		R	M	B	4s	6s	SR
WTS Porterfield*	c Smith b Morkel	6	8	8	1	0	75.00
PR Stirling	c Kallis b Morkel	10	15	11	2	0	90.90
EC Joyce	lbw b Botha	12	46	24	2	0	50.00
NJ O'Brien†	c †van Wyk b Kallis	10	23	16	0	1	62.50
GC Wilson	lbw b Peterson	31	60	48	4	1	64.58
KJ O'Brien	c Amla b Peterson	19	39	24	2	0	79.16
AR Cusack	c Smith b Peterson	7	23	11	1	0	63.63
JF Mooney	c †van Wyk b Kallis	14	49	28	1	0	50.00
DT Johnston	c †van Wyk b Duminy	12	14	16	0	1	75.00
GH Dockrell	c †van Wyk b Morkel	16	19	12	3	0	133.33
WB Rankin	not out	0	3	2	0	0	0.00
Extras	(w 4)	4					
Total	(all out; 33.2 overs; 154 mins)	141	(4.23 runs per over)				

Fall of wickets 1-8 (Porterfield, 1.6 ov), 2-19 (Stirling, 3.3 ov), 3-35 (NJ O'Brien, 8.5 ov), 4-51 (Joyce, 11.5 ov), 5-92 (KJ O'Brien, 21.3 ov), 6-92 (Wilson, 21.5 ov), 7-107 (Cusack, 25.5 ov), 8-123 (Johnston, 29.5 ov), 9-137 (Mooney, 32.4 ov), 10-141 (Dockrell, 33.2 ov)

Bowling	O	M	R	W	Econ	
DW Steyn	4	1	13	0	3.25	
M Morkel	5.2	0	33	3	6.18	(2w)
JH Kallis	6	1	20	2	3.33	
J Botha	8	0	32	1	4.00	(1w)
RJ Peterson	8	0	32	3	4.00	
JP Duminy	2	0	11	1	5.50	

South Africa won by 131 runs
Man of the match JP Duminy (South Africa)

Australia vs. Canada
16 March
M Chinnaswamy Stadium, Bangalore
Toss Canada chose to bat
Umpires BF Bowden (New Zealand) and AM Saheba

Canada innings		R	M	B	4s	6s	SR
H Patel	c Johnson b Watson	54	58	45	5	3	120.00
JM Davison	c †Haddin b Lee	14	19	12	3	0	116.66
ZE Surkari	b Tait	34	130	69	2	0	49.27
A Bagai*†	c †Haddin b Tait	39	74	55	6	0	70.90
AS Hansra	c Lee b Krejza	3	8	4	0	0	75.00
Rizwan Cheema	b Lee	2	12	2	0	0	100.00
NR Kumar	c Tait b Johnson	7	26	18	0	0	38.88
K Whatham	b Lee	18	57	41	2	0	43.90
HS Baidwan	c Ponting b Krejza	17	17	14	3	0	121.42
WD Balaji Rao	b Lee	5	10	12	0	0	41.66
H Osinde	not out	2	6	3	0	0	66.66
Extras	(lb 4, w 11, nb 1)	16					
Total	(all out; 45.4 overs; 213 mins)	211	(4.62 runs per over)				

Fall of wickets 1-41 (Davison, 3.5 ov), 2-82 (Patel, 11.3 ov), 3-150 (Bagai, 28.2 ov), 4-157 (Hansra, 29.6 ov), 5-157 (Surkari, 30.4 ov), 6-161 (Rizwan Cheema, 31.3 ov), 7-169 (Kumar, 36.3 ov), 8-195 (Baidwan, 41.2 ov), 9-204 (Balaji Rao, 43.6 ov), 10-211 (Whatham, 45.4 ov)

Bowling	O	M	R	W	Econ	
SW Tait	8	1	34	2	4.25	(1nb, 4w)
B Lee	8.4	0	46	4	5.30	(2w)
MG Johnson	10	0	43	1	4.30	(3w)
SR Watson	6	0	22	1	3.66	
JJ Krejza	10	0	44	2	4.40	(2w)
SPD Smith	3	0	18	0	6.00	

Australia innings		R	M	B	4s	6s	SR
SR Watson	c Osinde b Baidwan	94	129	90	9	4	104.44
BJ Haddin†	c †Bagai b Davison	88	124	84	11	2	104.76
RT Ponting*	c Davison b Osinde	7	30	15	0	0	46.66
MJ Clarke	not out	16	29	17	3	0	94.11
CL White	not out	4	3	3	1	0	133.33
Extras	(lb 1, w 2)	3					
Total	(3 wickets; 34.5 overs; 159 mins)	212	(6.08 runs per over)				

Did not bat MEK Hussey, SPD Smith, MG Johnson, B Lee, JJ Krejza, SW Tait
Fall of wickets 1-183 (Haddin, 28.5 ov), 2-185 (Watson, 29.3 ov), 3-207 (Ponting, 34.2 ov)

Bowling	O	M	R	W	Econ	
H Osinde	9.5	0	53	1	5.38	(2w)
HS Baidwan	10	1	41	1	4.10	
WD Balaji Rao	7	0	46	0	6.57	
Rizwan Cheema	3	0	23	0	7.66	
JM Davison	4	0	29	2	7.25	
H Patel	1	0	19	0	19.00	

Australia won by 7 wickets (with 91 balls remaining)
Man of the match SR Watson (Australia)

England vs. West Indies
17 March
MA Chidambaram Stadium, Chepauk, Chennai
Toss England chose to bat
Umpires SJ Davis (Australia) and BNJ Oxenford (Australia)

England innings		R	M	B	4s	6s	SR
AJ Strauss*	c Gayle b Russell	31	50	39	3	1	79.48
MJ Prior†	b Russell	21	36	21	3	0	100.00
IJL Trott	c Gayle b Bishoo	47	55	38	7	0	123.68
IR Bell	b Roach	27	58	48	1	0	56.25
EJG Morgan	c †Thomas b Bishoo	7	22	13	0	0	53.84
RS Bopara	b Russell	4	27	16	0	0	25.00
LJ Wright	c Russell b Bishoo	44	72	57	5	0	77.19
JC Tredwell	run out (†Thomas/Pollard)	9	32	20	0	0	45.00
TT Bresnan	not out	20	39	27	2	0	74.07
GP Swann	b Russell	8	14	8	1	0	100.00
CT Tremlett	c †Thomas b Roach	3	6	7	0	0	42.85
Extras	(b 1, lb 4, w 15, nb 2)	22					
Total	(all out; 48.4 overs; 210 mins)	243	(4.99 runs per over)				

Fall of wickets 1-48 (Prior, 9.1 ov), 2-79 (Strauss, 11.5 ov), 3-121 (Trott, 21.6 ov), 4-134 (Bell, 26.1 ov), 5-134 (Morgan, 27.2 ov), 6-151 (Bopara, 32.2 ov), 7-192 (Tredwell, 39.2 ov), 8-216 (Wright, 43.4 ov), 9-238 (Swann, 47.1 ov), 10-243 (Tremlett, 48.4 ov)

Bowling	O	M	R	W	Econ	
KAJ Roach	9.4	2	34	2	3.51	(2nb, 1w)
SJ Benn	10	0	56	0	5.60	(2w)
AD Russell	8	0	49	4	6.12	(3w)
DJG Sammy	3	0	28	0	9.33	
D Bishoo	10	0	34	3	3.40	
KA Pollard	8	0	37	0	4.62	(1w)

West Indies innings		R	M	B	4s	6s	SR
DS Smith	st †Prior b Tredwell	10	37	27	0	0	37.03
CH Gayle	lbw b Tredwell	43	27	21	8	1	204.76
DJG Sammy*	b Bopara	41	45	29	2	3	141.37
DM Bravo	c Strauss b Tredwell	5	15	15	1	0	33.33
DC Thomas†	b Bopara	9	30	20	1	0	45.00
RR Sarwan	c Bell b Swann	31	114	68	3	0	45.58
KA Pollard	lbw b Swann	24	33	27	1	2	88.88
AD Russell	lbw b Tredwell	49	59	46	2	3	106.52
SJ Benn	run out (Trott/†Prior)	2	19	12	0	0	16.66
KAJ Roach	c Tremlett b Swann	0	1	2	0	0	0.00
D Bishoo	not out	0	6	1	0	0	0.00
Extras	(lb 8, w 3)	11					
Total	(all out; 44.4 overs; 197 mins)	225	(5.03 runs per over)				

Fall of wickets 1-58 (Gayle, 6.5 ov), 2-67 (Smith, 8.6 ov), 3-91 (Bravo, 12.6 ov), 4-113 (Sammy, 17.1 ov), 5-118 (Thomas, 19.4 ov), 6-150 (Pollard, 27.4 ov), 7-222 (Russell, 41.2 ov), 8-223 (Sarwan, 43.1 ov), 9-223 (Roach, 43.3 ov), 10-225 (Benn, 44.4 ov)

Bowling	O	M	R	W	Econ	
TT Bresnan	7	1	46	0	6.57	
GP Swann	10	1	36	3	3.60	(1w)
CT Tremlett	5	0	47	0	9.40	(1w)
JC Tredwell	10	2	48	4	4.80	(1w)
RS Bopara	8.4	2	22	2	2.53	
LJ Wright	4	0	18	0	4.50	

England won by 18 runs
Man of the match JC Tredwell (England)

Ireland vs. Netherlands
18 March
Eden Gardens, Kolkata
Toss Ireland chose to field
Umpires BR Doctrove (West Indies) and IJ Gould (England)

Netherlands innings		R	M	B	4s	6s	SR
ES Szwarczynski	c †NJ O'Brien b Johnston	1	8	4	0	0	25.00
W Barresi	lbw b Stirling	44	61	49	4	2	89.79
TLW Cooper	c Porterfield b Rankin	5	7	5	1	0	100.00
RN ten Doeschate	c Mooney b Stirling	106	166	108	13	1	98.14
AN Kervezee	c KJ O'Brien b Mooney	12	34	16	2	0	75.00
PW Borren*	c Porterfield b Mooney	84	108	82	10	0	102.43
AF Buurman†	run out (†NJ O'Brien)	26	49	30	4	0	86.66
Mudassar Bukhari	run out (Mooney/†NJ O'Brien)	11	22	8	0	1	137.50
PM Seelaar	run out (Mooney)	0	1	1	0	0	0.00
Adeel Raja	run out (Joyce/KJ O'Brien)	0	1	0	0	0	-
BP Loots	not out	0	1	0	0	0	-
Extras	(b 1, lb 8, w 5, nb 3)	17					
Total	(all out; 50 overs; 234 mins)	306	(6.12 runs per over)				

Fall of wickets 0-7* (Barresi, retired not out, 1.3 ov), 1-7 (Szwarczynski, 1.3 ov), 2-12 (Cooper, 2.3 ov), 3-53 (Kervezee, 10.1 ov), 4-113 (Barresi, 21.5 ov), 5-234 (ten Doeschate, 39.5 ov), 6-287 (Borren, 46.5 ov), 7-305 (Buurman, 49.3 ov), 8-305 (Seelaar, 49.4 ov), 9-305 (Adeel Raja, 49.5 ov), 10-306 (Mudassar Bukhari, 49.6 ov)

Bowling	O	M	R	W	Econ	
WB Rankin	9	0	74	1	8.22	(3nb, 3w)
DT Johnston	10	1	50	1	5.00	
JF Mooney	10	0	59	2	5.90	
GH Dockrell	3.4	0	15	0	4.09	
PR Stirling	10	0	51	2	5.10	
AR Cusack	2.2	0	15	0	6.42	
KJ O'Brien	5	0	33	0	6.60	(2w)

Ireland innings		R	M	B	4s	6s	SR
WTS Porterfield*	c †Buurman b Cooper	68	116	93	10	0	73.11
PR Stirling	c Kervezee b Seelaar	101	119	72	14	2	140.27
EC Joyce	c †Buurman b Cooper	28	45	33	3	0	84.84
NJ O'Brien†	not out	57	83	58	7	0	98.27
GC Wilson	c †Buurman b ten Doeschate	27	26	21	2	2	128.57
KJ O'Brien	not out	15	13	9	0	2	166.66
Extras	(lb 10, w 1)	11					
Total	(4 wickets; 47.4 overs; 203 mins)	307	(6.44 runs per over)				

Did not bat AR Cusack, DT Johnston, JF Mooney, GH Dockrell, WB Rankin
Fall of wickets 1-177 (Porterfield, 26.6 ov), 2-179 (Stirling, 27.3 ov), 3-233 (Joyce, 38.1 ov), 4-279 (Wilson, 44.3 ov)

Bowling	O	M	R	W	Econ	
Mudassar Bukhari	7	0	42	0	6.00	
Adeel Raja	8	1	44	0	5.50	
BP Loots	2	0	29	0	14.50	
RN ten Doeschate	9	1	58	1	6.44	(1w)
PM Seelaar	9.4	1	55	1	5.68	
PW Borren	5	0	38	0	7.60	
TLW Cooper	7	1	31	2	4.42	

Ireland won by 6 wickets (with 14 balls remaining)
Man of the match PR Stirling (Ireland)

New Zealand vs. Sri Lanka

18 March
Wankhede Stadium, Mumbai
Toss Sri Lanka chose to bat
Umpires Asad Rauf (Pakistan) and RA Kettleborough (England)

Sri Lanka innings		R	M	B	4s	6s	SR
WU Tharanga	run out (Southee)	3	13	7	0	0	42.85
TM Dilshan	c Oram b Southee	3	22	15	0	0	20.00
KC Sangakkara*†	b NL McCullum	111	186	128	12	2	86.71
DPMD Jayawardene	lbw b Southee	66	149	90	6	0	73.33
AD Mathews	not out	41	67	35	4	0	117.14
TT Samaraweera	c †BB McCullum b Styris	5	8	8	0	0	62.50
LPC Silva	c & b NL McCullum	3	5	5	0	0	60.00
KMDN Kulasekara	c Guptill b Southee	1	7	6	0	0	16.66
SL Malinga	c †BB McCullum b Oram	6	4	4	0	1	150.00
M Muralitharan	run out (Oram/Guptill/NL McCullum)	7	7	3	0	1	233.33
BAW Mendis	not out	0	2	2	0	0	0.00
Extras	(lb 4, w 12, nb 3)	19					
Total	(9 wickets; 50 overs; 235 mins)	265	(5.30 runs per over)				

Fall of wickets 1-13 (Tharanga, 2.6 ov), 2-19 (Dilshan, 4.3 ov), 3-164 (Jayawardene, 36.1 ov), 4-210 (Sangakkara, 41.4 ov), 5-219 (Samaraweera, 44.1 ov), 6-224 (Silva, 45.4 ov), 7-232 (Kulasekara, 46.6 ov), 8-239 (Malinga, 47.5 ov), 9-260 (Muralitharan, 49.2 ov)

Bowling	O	M	R	W	Econ	
TG Southee	10	0	63	3	6.30	(5w)
JDP Oram	10	1	57	1	5.70	(1nb, 1w)
HK Bennett	4.1	0	16	0	3.84	(1nb, 1w)
JD Ryder	3.5	0	18	0	4.69	(1nb, 1w)
JEC Franklin	3	0	11	0	3.66	
SB Styris	8	0	44	1	5.50	
NL McCullum	10	0	48	2	4.80	
KS Williamson	1	0	4	0	4.00	

New Zealand innings		R	M	B	4s	6s	SR
MJ Guptill	lbw b Kulasekara	13	36	23	1	0	56.52
BB McCullum†	c Jayawardene b Mathews	14	30	16	2	0	87.50
JD Ryder	c †Sangakkara b Mendis	19	55	23	2	0	82.60
LRPL Taylor*	lbw b Muralitharan	33	72	55	3	1	60.00
KS Williamson	st †Sangakkara b Muralitharan	5	12	8	0	0	62.50
SB Styris	c & b Muralitharan	6	21	10	0	0	60.00
JEC Franklin	c Dilshan b Muralitharan	20	44	29	2	0	68.96
NL McCullum	c Jayawardene b Dilshan	4	13	8	0	0	50.00
JDP Oram	not out	20	38	27	2	0	74.07
TG Southee	lbw b Mendis	8	9	8	1	0	100.00
HK Bennett	b Malinga	0	8	4	0	0	0.00
Extras	(lb 4, w 6, nb 1)	11					
Total	(all out; 35 overs; 173 mins)	153	(4.37 runs per over)				

Fall of wickets 1-29 (BB McCullum, 6.2 ov), 2-33 (Guptill, 7.1 ov), 3-82 (Ryder, 16.5 ov), 4-88 (Williamson, 19.2 ov), 5-93 (Taylor, 21.1 ov), 6-102 (Styris, 23.5 ov), 7-115 (NL McCullum, 26.5 ov), 8-129 (Franklin, 31.3 ov), 9-144 (Southee, 33.4 ov), 10-153 (Bennett, 34.6 ov)

Bowling	O	M	R	W	Econ	
SL Malinga	5	0	38	1	7.60	(3w)
KMDN Kulasekara	7	0	19	1	2.71	(2w)
AD Mathews	3	0	19	1	6.33	
BAW Mendis	6	0	24	2	4.00	(1w)
TM Dilshan	6	0	24	1	4.00	
M Muralitharan	8	0	25	4	3.12	(1nb)

Sri Lanka won by 112 runs
Man of the match KC Sangakkara (Sri Lanka)

Bangladesh vs. South Africa
19 March
Shere Bangla National Stadium, Mirpur
Toss South Africa chose to bat
Umpires Aleem Dar (Pakistan) and **DJ Harper** (Australia)

South Africa innings		R	M	B	4s	6s	SR
HM Amla	b Abdur Razzak	51	93	59	6	0	86.44
GC Smith*	st †Mushfiqur Rahim b Mahmudullah	45	86	68	4	0	66.17
JH Kallis	c & b Shakib Al Hasan	69	88	76	5	1	90.78
JP Duminy	c †Mushfiqur Rahim b Rubel Hossain	17	26	22	1	0	77.27
F du Plessis	c Tamim Iqbal b Rubel Hossain	52	73	52	4	1	100.00
MN van Wyk†	b Shakib Al Hasan	5	13	5	0	0	100.00
J Botha	run out (Rubel Hossain)	12	15	6	2	0	200.00
RJ Peterson	not out	22	15	9	4	0	244.44
WD Parnell	b Rubel Hossain	0	2	1	0	0	0.00
LL Tsotsobe	not out	4	2	2	1	0	200.00
Extras	(lb 3, w 4)	7					
Total	(8 wickets; 50 overs; 212 mins)	284	(5.68 runs per over)				

Did not bat Imran Tahir
Fall of wickets 1-98 (Smith, 20.4 ov), 2-107 (Amla, 22.3 ov), 3-141 (Duminy, 29.6 ov), 4-223 (Kallis, 44.3 ov), 5-245 (van Wyk, 46.4 ov), 6-249 (du Plessis, 47.3 ov), 7-273 (Botha, 49.1 ov), 8-280 (Parnell, 49.4 ov)

Bowling	O	M	R	W	Econ	
Shafiul Islam	5	0	44	0	8.80	(1w)
Rubel Hossain	8	0	56	3	7.00	
Abdur Razzak	10	1	47	1	4.70	(1w)
Naeem Islam	7	0	42	0	6.00	(1w)
Mahmudullah	10	0	46	1	4.60	(1w)
Al Hasan	10	0	46	2	4.60	

Bangladesh innings		R	M	B	4s	6s	SR
Tamim Iqbal	c †van Wyk b Tsotsobe	5	13	14	1	0	35.71
Imrul Kayes	b Tsotsobe	4	22	15	1	0	26.66
Junaid Siddique	lbw b Botha	2	14	7	0	0	28.57
Shahriar Nafees	b Tsotsobe	5	12	12	1	0	41.66
Mushfiqur Rahim†	c Smith b Peterson	3	34	21	0	0	14.28
Shakib Al Hasan*	c †van Wyk b Peterson	30	63	49	4	0	61.22
Mahmudullah	run out (Botha/†van Wyk)	5	26	17	0	0	29.41
Naeem Islam	b Peterson	8	24	20	1	0	40.00
Shafiul Islam	b Peterson	0	1	2	0	0	0.00
Abdur Razzak	c Peterson b Imran Tahir	0	3	2	0	0	0.00
Rubel Hossain	not out	8	10	9	2	0	88.88
Extras	(lb 5, w 3)	8					
Total	(all out; 28 overs; 116 mins)	78	(2.78 runs per over)				

Fall of wickets 1-14 (Tamim Iqbal, 3.3 ov), 2-15 (Imrul Kayes, 5.4 ov), 3-21 (Junaid Siddique, 6.6 ov), 4-21 (Shahriar Nafees, 7.6 ov), 5-36 (Mushfiqur Rahim, 15.1 ov), 6-58 (Mahmudullah, 21.3 ov), 7-61 (Shakib Al Hasan, 23.4 ov), 8-61 (Shafiul Islam, 23.6 ov), 9-62 (Abdur Razzak, 24.6 ov), 10-78 (Naeem Islam, 27.6 ov)

Bowling	O	M	R	W	Econ	
J Botha	7	1	23	1	3.28	
LL Tsotsobe	5	2	14	3	2.80	(1w)
WD Parnell	4	1	4	0	1.00	
RJ Peterson	7	3	12	4	1.71	
Imran Tahir	5	0	20	1	4.00	(2w)

South Africa won by 206 runs
Man of the match LL Tsotsobe (South Africa)

Australia vs. Pakistan

19 March
R Premadasa Stadium, Colombo
Toss Australia chose to bat
Umpires M Erasmus (South Africa) and AL Hill (New Zealand)

Australia innings		R	M	B	4s	6s	SR
SR Watson	b Umar Gul	9	24	16	1	0	56.25
BJ Haddin†	c †Kamran Akmal b Wahab Riaz	42	102	80	3	1	52.50
RT Ponting*	c †Kamran Akmal b Mohammad Hafeez	19	57	33	2	0	57.57
MJ Clarke	b Abdul Razzaq	34	59	48	2	0	70.83
CL White	run out (Misbah-ul-Haq/†Kamran Akmal)	8	22	18	0	0	44.44
MEK Hussey	c Misbah-ul-Haq b Abdul Rehman	12	29	22	0	0	54.54
SPD Smith	b Shahid Afridi	25	46	32	1	0	78.12
MG Johnson	c †Kamran Akmal b Abdul Razzaq	0	4	3	0	0	0.00
JJ Krejza	b Umar Gul	7	22	19	0	0	36.84
B Lee	c Misbah-ul-Haq b Umar Gul	5	11	8	1	0	62.50
SW Tait	not out	0	5	1	0	0	0.00
Extras	(lb 5, w 10)	15					
Total	(all out; 46.4 overs; 195 mins)	176	(3.77 runs per over)				

Fall of wickets 1-12 (Watson, 4.3 ov), 2-75 (Ponting, 18.4 ov), 3-90 (Haddin, 23.4 ov), 4-117 (White, 30.1 ov), 5-134 (Clarke, 34.4 ov), 6-144 (Hussey, 37.4 ov), 7-147 (Johnson, 38.4 ov), 8-169 (Krejza, 44.3 ov), 9-176 (Smith, 45.5 ov), 10-176 (Lee, 46.4 ov)

Bowling	O	M	R	W	Econ	
Umar Gul	7.4	1	30	3	3.91	(1w)
Abdur Rehman	10	0	34	1	3.40	(1w)
Shahid Afridi	9	0	34	1	3.77	(1w)
Wahab Riaz	6	0	39	1	6.50	(3w)
Mohammad Hafeez	10	0	26	1	2.60	
Abdul Razzaq	4	0	8	2	2.00	

Pakistan innings		R	M	B	4s	6s	SR
Kamran Akmal†	lbw b Lee	23	48	27	5	0	85.18
Mohammad Hafeez	c & b Lee	5	12	8	1	0	62.50
Asad Shafiq	c Watson b Johnson	46	148	81	5	0	56.79
Younis Khan	c †Haddin b Lee	31	66	42	4	0	73.80
Misbah-ul-Haq	c †Haddin b Lee	0	2	1	0	0	0.00
Umar Akmal	not out	44	80	59	4	1	74.57
Shahid Afridi*	c Lee b Krejza	2	3	4	0	0	50.00
Abdul Razzaq	not out	20	33	24	2	0	83.33
Extras	(b 2, lb 1, w 4)	7					
Total	(6 wickets; 41 overs; 199 mins)	178	(4.34 runs per over)				

Did not bat Abdur Rehman, Umar Gul, Wahab Riaz
Fall of wickets 1-12 (Mohammad Hafeez, 2.4 ov), 2-45 (Kamran Akmal, 8.4 ov), 3-98 (Younis Khan, 22.4 ov), 4-98 (Misbah-ul-Haq, 22.5 ov), 5-139 (Asad Shafiq, 31.6 ov), 6-142 (Shahid Afridi, 32.5 ov)

Bowling	O	M	R	W	Econ	
B Lee	8	1	28	4	3.50	
SW Tait	8	1	37	0	4.62	(3w)
MG Johnson	9	1	40	1	4.44	(1w)
SR Watson	6	0	26	0	4.33	
JJ Krejza	10	0	44	1	4.40	

Pakistan won by 4 wickets (with 54 balls remaining)
Man of the match Umar Akmal (Pakistan)

Kenya vs. Zimbabwe
20 March
Eden Gardens, Kolkata
Toss Zimbabwe chose to bat
Umpires EAR de Silva (Sri Lanka) and HDPK Dharmasena (Sri Lanka)

Zimbabwe innings		R	M	B	4s	6s	SR
BRM Taylor	c Ngoche b Otieno	26	41	36	5	0	72.22
RW Chakabva	c †DO Obuya b Odhiambo	9	36	22	1	0	40.90
T Taibu†	lbw b Ngoche	53	103	74	7	0	71.62
V Sibanda	run out (CO Obuya)	61	82	57	7	1	107.01
CR Ervine	b Otieno	66	89	54	9	1	122.22
E Chigumbura*	c Mishra b Ongondo	38	68	41	3	2	92.68
GA Lamb	not out	17	14	10	1	1	170.00
P Utseya	not out	19	9	6	3	1	316.66
Extras	(b 2, lb 3, w 14)	19					
Total	(6 wickets; 50 overs; 224 mins)	**308**	(6.16 runs per over)				

Did not bat AG Cremer, RW Price, CB Mpofu
Fall of wickets 1-32 (Chakabva, 8.6 ov), 2-36 (Taylor, 9.4 ov), 3-146 (Sibanda, 29.1 ov), 4-165 (Taibu, 32.4 ov), 5-270 (Chigumbura, 46.6 ov), 6-276 (Ervine, 47.6 ov)

Bowling	O	M	R	W	Econ	
PJ Ongondo	10	0	53	1	5.30	(3w)
E Otieno	10	0	61	2	6.10	
NN Odhiambo	10	1	58	1	5.80	(3w)
JO Ngoche	10	0	68	1	6.80	(1w)
CO Obuya	3	0	14	0	4.66	
SO Tikolo	7	0	49	0	7.00	(2w)

Kenya innings		R	M	B	4s	6s	SR
AA Obanda	lbw b Price	23	51	36	4	0	63.88
DO Obuya†	lbw b Mpofu	0	4	2	0	0	0.00
CO Obuya	run out (Sibanda)	1	12	6	0	0	16.66
SO Tikolo*	lbw b Price	10	16	14	2	0	71.42
T Mishra	c Cremer b Utseya	4	11	9	1	0	44.44
TM Odoyo	lbw b Lamb	14	35	29	2	0	48.27
RR Patel	c Chakabva b Lamb	24	50	37	3	0	64.86
NN Odhiambo	not out	44	67	47	5	0	93.61
PJ Ongondo	lbw b Cremer	6	2	2	0	1	300.00
E Otieno	run out (Chigumbura)	5	24	13	0	0	38.46
JO Ngoche	c Mpofu b Cremer	9	19	21	0	1	42.85
Extras	(lb 4, w 3)	7					
Total	(all out; 36 overs; 150 mins)	**147**	(4.08 runs per over)				

Fall of wickets 1-3 (DO Obuya, 0.5 ov), 2-10 (CO Obuya, 3.3 ov), 3-27 (Tikolo, 7.3 ov), 4-44 (Mishra, 10.3 ov), 5-44 (Obanda, 11.4 ov), 6-73 (Odoyo, 19.5 ov), 7-95 (Patel, 24.6 ov), 8-101 (Ongondo, 25.2 ov), 9-124 (Otieno, 31.2 ov), 10-147 (Ngoche, 35.6 ov)

Bowling	O	M	R	W	Econ	
CB Mpofu	6	0	27	1	4.50	(2w)
RW Price	7	1	20	2	2.85	
P Utseya	9	0	47	1	5.22	
GA Lamb	7	0	21	2	3.00	
AG Cremer	7	0	28	2	4.00	(1w)

Zimbabwe won by 161 runs
Man of the match CR Ervine (Zimbabwe)

India vs. West Indies
20 March
MA Chidambaram Stadium, Chepauk, Chennai
Toss India chose to bat
Umpires SJ Davis (Australia) and SJA Taufel (Australia)

India innings		R	M	B	4s	6s	SR
G Gambhir	c Russell b Rampaul	22	34	26	4	0	84.61
SR Tendulkar	c †Thomas b Rampaul	2	4	4	0	0	50.00
V Kohli	b Rampaul	59	128	76	5	0	77.63
Yuvraj Singh	c & b Pollard	113	163	123	10	2	91.86
MS Dhoni*†	st †Thomas b Bishoo	22	41	30	1	0	73.33
SK Raina	c Rampaul b Sammy	4	14	8	0	0	50.00
YK Pathan	b Rampaul	11	16	10	1	0	110.00
Harbhajan Singh	c Pollard b Russell	3	16	6	0	0	50.00
R Ashwin	not out	10	14	7	1	0	142.85
Z Khan	b Rampaul	5	4	3	1	0	166.66
MM Patel	b Russell	1	1	2	0	0	50.00
Extras	(b 5, lb 2, w 9)	16					
Total	(all out; 49.1 overs; 222 mins)	268	(5.45 runs per over)				

Fall of wickets 1-8 (Tendulkar, 0.6 ov), 2-51 (Gambhir, 8.3 ov), 3-173 (Kohli, 32.2 ov), 4-218 (Dhoni, 41.4 ov), 5-232 (Raina, 43.5 ov), 6-240 (Yuvraj Singh, 44.6 ov), 7-251 (Pathan, 46.4 ov), 8-259 (Harbhajan Singh, 47.5 ov), 9-267 (Khan, 48.5 ov), 10-268 (Patel, 49.1 ov)

Bowling	O	M	R	W	Econ	
R Rampaul	10	0	51	5	5.10	(1w)
SJ Benn	4	0	32	0	8.00	
AD Russell	9.1	1	46	2	5.01	(2w)
DJG Sammy	6	0	35	1	5.83	(1w)
D Bishoo	10	0	48	1	4.80	
KA Pollard	10	0	49	1	4.90	(1w)

West Indies innings		R	M	B	4s	6s	SR
DS Smith	b Khan	81	117	97	7	1	83.50
KA Edwards	lbw b Ashwin	17	26	17	1	1	100.00
DM Bravo	c Harbhajan Singh b Raina	22	35	29	1	1	75.86
RR Sarwan	c Ashwin b Khan	39	111	68	3	0	57.35
KA Pollard	c Pathan b Harbhajan Singh	1	6	3	0	0	33.33
DC Thomas†	st †Dhoni b Yuvraj Singh	2	12	8	0	0	25.00
DJG Sammy*	run out (Raina/Patel)	2	7	4	0	0	50.00
AD Russell	c Pathan b Yuvraj Singh	0	5	5	0	0	0.00
SJ Benn	c Patel b Khan	3	15	12	0	0	25.00
D Bishoo	not out	6	13	11	1	0	54.54
R Rampaul	b Ashwin	1	7	4	0	0	25.00
Extras	(lb 8, w 6)	14					
Total	(all out; 43 overs; 181 mins)	188	(4.37 runs per over)				

Fall of wickets 1-34 (Edwards, 6.2 ov), 2-91 (Bravo, 16.6 ov), 3-154 (Smith, 30.3 ov), 4-157 (Pollard, 31.5 ov), 5-160 (Thomas, 34.2 ov), 6-162 (Sammy, 35.3 ov), 7-165 (Russell, 36.6 ov), 8-179 (Benn, 39.6 ov), 9-182 (Sarwan, 41.1 ov), 10-188 (Rampaul, 42.6 ov)

Bowling	O	M	R	W	Econ	
R Ashwin	10	0	41	2	4.10	(1w)
Z Khan	6	0	26	3	4.33	(2w)
Harbhajan Singh	9	1	35	1	3.88	(1w)
YK Pathan	7	0	28	0	4.00	
SK Raina	2	0	12	1	6.00	
Yuvraj Singh	4	0	18	2	4.50	
MM Patel	5	0	20	0	4.00	(1w)

India won by 80 runs
Man of the match Yuvraj Singh (India)

Pakistan vs. West Indies
23 March
Shere Bangla National Stadium, Mirpur
Toss West Indies chose to bat
Umpires BF Bowden (New Zealand) and SJ Davis (Australia)

West Indies innings		R	M	B	4s	6s	SR
DS Smith	lbw b Mohammad Hafeez	7	25	14	1	0	50.00
CH Gayle	c Shahid Afridi b Umar Gul	8	12	9	2	0	88.88
RR Sarwan	c Umar Akmal b Shahid Afridi	24	92	68	2	0	35.29
DM Bravo	lbw b Mohammad Hafeez	0	2	3	0	0	0.00
S Chanderpaul	not out	44	156	106	0	1	41.50
KA Pollard	c †Kamran Akmal b Shahid Afridi	1	9	7	0	0	14.28
DC Thomas†	lbw b Shahid Afridi	0	1	1	0	0	0.00
DJG Sammy*	lbw b Saeed Ajmal	1	3	3	0	0	33.33
D Bishoo	b Saeed Ajmal	0	3	3	0	0	0.00
KAJ Roach	c Younis Khan b Abdul Razzaq	16	60	43	2	0	37.20
R Rampaul	b Shahid Afridi	0	4	5	0	0	0.00
Extras	(lb 2, w 7, nb 2)	11					
Total	(all out; 43.3 overs; 188 mins)	112	(2.57 runs per over)				

Fall of wickets 1-14 (Gayle, 2.5 ov), 2-16 (Smith, 5.1 ov), 3-16 (Bravo, 5.4 ov), 4-58 (Sarwan, 24.1 ov), 5-69 (Pollard, 26.4 ov), 6-69 (Thomas, 26.5 ov), 7-71 (Sammy, 27.2 ov), 8-71 (Bishoo, 27.5 ov), 9-111 (Roach, 42.2 ov), 10-112 (Rampaul, 43.3 ov)

Bowling	O	M	R	W	Econ	
Umar Gul	7	1	13	1	1.85	
Mohammad Hafeez	10	3	16	2	1.60	(2w)
Wahab Riaz	6	0	29	0	4.83	(1nb, 2w)
Shahid Afridi	9.3	1	30	4	3.15	(1w)
Saeed Ajmal	8	1	18	2	2.25	(1w)
Abdul Razzaq	3	1	4	1	1.33	(1w)

Pakistan innings		R	M	B	4s	6s	SR
Kamran Akmal†	not out	47	88	61	7	0	77.04
Mohammad Hafeez	not out	61	88	64	10	0	95.31
Extras	(lb 4, w 1)	5					
Total	(0 wickets; 20.5 overs; 88 mins)	113	(5.42 runs per over)				

Did not bat Asad Shafiq, Younis Khan, Misbah-ul-Haq, Umar Akmal, Abdul Razzaq, Shahid Afridi*, Umar Gul, Wahab Riaz, Saeed Ajmal

Bowling	O	M	R	W	Econ	
KAJ Roach	5.5	0	39	0	6.68	
R Rampaul	5	1	28	0	5.60	(1w)
D Bishoo	5	1	24	0	4.80	
DJG Sammy	5	1	18	0	3.60	

Pakistan won by 10 wickets (with 175 balls remaining)
Man of the match Mohammad Hafeez (Pakistan)

QUARTER-FINAL

India vs. Australia
24 March
Sardar Patel Stadium, Motera, Ahmedabad
Toss Australia chose to bat
Umpires M Erasmus (South Africa) and IJ Gould (England)

Australia innings		R	M	B	4s	6s	SR
SR Watson	b Ashwin	25	39	38	5	0	65.78
BJ Haddin†	c Raina b Yuvraj Singh	53	95	62	6	1	85.48
RT Ponting*	c Khan b Ashwin	104	172	118	7	1	88.13
MJ Clarke	c Khan b Yuvraj Singh	8	30	19	0	0	42.10
MEK Hussey	b Khan	3	15	9	0	0	33.33
CL White	c & b Khan	12	36	22	0	0	54.54
DJ Hussey	not out	38	44	26	3	1	146.15
MG Johnson	not out	6	7	6	0	0	100.00
Extras	(lb 2, w 9)	11					
Total	(6 wickets; 50 overs; 220 mins)	260	(5.20 runs per over)				

Did not bat B Lee, JJ Krejza, SW Tait
Fall of wickets 1-40 (Watson, 9.6 ov), 2-110 (Haddin, 22.5 ov), 3-140 (Clarke, 30.4 ov), 4-150 (MEK Hussey, 33.3 ov), 5-190 (White, 41.2 ov), 6-245 (Ponting, 48.3 ov)

Bowling	O	M	R	W	Econ	
R Ashwin	10	0	52	2	5.20	(1w)
Z Khan	10	0	53	2	5.30	
Harbhajan Singh	10	0	50	0	5.00	(4w)
MM Patel	7	0	44	0	6.28	
Yuvraj Singh	10	0	44	2	4.40	
SR Tendulkar	2	0	9	0	4.50	
V Kohli	1	0	6	0	6.00	

India innings		R	M	B	4s	6s	SR
V Sehwag	c MEK Hussey b Watson	15	46	22	2	0	68.18
SR Tendulkar	c †Haddin b Tait	53	93	68	7	0	77.94
G Gambhir	run out (White/DJ Hussey)	50	116	64	2	0	78.12
V Kohli	c Clarke b DJ Hussey	24	38	33	1	0	72.72
Yuvraj Singh	not out	57	90	65	8	0	87.69
MS Dhoni*†	c Clarke b Lee	7	19	8	1	0	87.50
SK Raina	not out	34	48	28	2	1	121.42
Extras	(lb 3, w 16, nb 2)	21					
Total	(5 wickets; 47.4 overs; 232 mins)	261	(5.47 runs per over)				

Did not bat R Ashwin, Harbhajan Singh, Z Khan, MM Patel
Fall of wickets 1-44 (Sehwag, 8.1 ov), 2-94 (Tendulkar, 18.1 ov), 3-143 (Kohli, 28.3 ov), 4-168 (Gambhir, 33.2 ov), 5-187 (Dhoni, 37.3 ov)

Bowling	O	M	R	W	Econ	
B Lee	8.4	1	45	1	5.19	(3w)
SW Tait	7	0	52	1	7.42	(2nb, 6w)
MG Johnson	8	0	41	0	5.12	(2w)
SR Watson	7	0	37	1	5.28	(1w)
JJ Krejza	9	0	45	0	5.00	
MJ Clarke	3	0	19	0	6.33	
DJ Hussey	5	0	19	1	3.80	

India won by 5 wickets (with 14 balls remaining)
Man of the match Yuvraj Singh (India)

New Zealand vs. South Africa
25 March
Shere Bangla National Stadium, Mirpur
Toss New Zealand chose to bat
Umpires Aleem Dar (Pakistan) and RJ Tucker (Australia)

New Zealand innings		R	M	B	4s	6s	SR
MJ Guptill	c Botha b Steyn	1	24	14	0	0	7.14
BB McCullum†	c & b Peterson	4	7	4	0	0	100.00
JD Ryder	c sub (CA Ingram) b Imran Tahir	83	157	121	8	0	68.59
LRPL Taylor	c Kallis b Imran Tahir	43	113	72	1	1	59.72
SB Styris	b Morkel	16	19	17	3	0	94.11
KS Williamson	not out	38	63	41	1	1	92.68
NL McCullum	c Duminy b Steyn	6	29	18	0	0	33.33
JDP Oram	b Morkel	7	14	6	1	0	116.66
DL Vettori*	b Morkel	6	4	4	1	0	150.00
LJ Woodcock	not out	3	8	3	0	0	100.00
Extras	(b 4, lb 4, w 6)	14					
Total	(8 wickets; 50 overs; 220 mins)	221	(4.42 runs per over)				

Did not bat TG Southee
Fall of wickets 1-5 (BB McCullum, 2.1 ov), 2-16 (Guptill, 5.6 ov), 3-130 (Taylor, 32.6 ov), 4-153 (Styris, 37.2 ov), 5-156 (Ryder, 38.5 ov), 6-188 (NL McCullum, 45.3 ov), 7-204 (Oram, 48.1 ov), 8-210 (Vettori, 48.5 ov)

Bowling	O	M	R	W	Econ	
RJ Peterson	9	0	49	1	5.44	
DW Steyn	10	0	42	2	4.20	(2w)
J Botha	9	0	29	0	3.22	(1w)
M Morkel	8	0	46	3	5.75	
Imran Tahir	9	0	32	2	3.55	(1w)
JH Kallis	3	1	6	0	2.00	
JP Duminy	2	0	9	0	4.50	(1w)

South Africa innings		R	M	B	4s	6s	SR
HM Amla	c Vettori b NL McCullum	7	4	5	1	0	140.00
GC Smith*	c sub (JM How) b Oram	28	59	34	2	0	82.35
JH Kallis	c Oram b Southee	47	96	75	3	0	62.66
AB de Villiers†	run out (Guptill/†BB McCullum)	35	63	40	4	0	87.50
JP Duminy	b NL McCullum	3	18	12	0	0	25.00
F du Plessis	c Southee b Oram	36	70	43	3	1	83.72
J Botha	b Oram	2	18	10	0	0	20.00
RJ Peterson	c †BB McCullum b Oram	0	9	5	0	0	0.00
DW Steyn	c Oram b NL McCullum	8	14	18	1	0	44.44
M Morkel	c sub (JM How) b Woodcock	3	30	17	0	0	17.64
Imran Tahir	not out	0	4	1	0	0	0.00
Extras	(lb 2, w 1)	3					
Total	(all out; 43.2 overs; 192 mins)	172	(3.96 runs per over)				

Fall of wickets 1-8 (Amla, 0.6 ov), 2-69 (Smith, 14.2 ov), 3-108 (Kallis, 24.1 ov), 4-121 (Duminy, 27.4 ov), 5-121 (de Villiers, 27.6 ov), 6-128 (Botha, 32.5 ov), 7-132 (Peterson, 34.2 ov), 8-146 (Steyn, 37.4 ov), 9-172 (du Plessis, 42.5 ov), 10-172 (Morkel, 43.2 ov)

Bowling	O	M	R	W	Econ	
NL McCullum	10	1	24	3	2.40	
DL Vettori	10	0	39	0	3.90	
TG Southee	9	0	44	1	4.88	
JDP Oram	9	1	39	4	4.33	
LJ Woodcock	5.2	0	24	1	4.50	(1w)

New Zealand won by 49 runs
Man of the match JDP Oram (New Zealand)

Sri Lanka vs. England

26 March
R Premadasa Stadium, Colombo
Toss England chose to bat
Umpires BR Doctrove (West Indies) and SJA Taufel (Australia)

England innings		R	M	B	4s	6s	SR
AJ Strauss*	b Dilshan	5	30	19	0	0	26.31
IR Bell	c Samaraweera b Mathews	25	36	32	3	0	78.12
IJL Trott	c Jayawardene b Muralitharan	86	172	115	2	0	74.78
RS Bopara	lbw b Muralitharan	31	70	56	1	0	55.35
EJG Morgan	c Mathews b Malinga	50	66	55	4	0	90.90
GP Swann	lbw b Mendis	0	2	1	0	0	0.00
MJ Prior†	not out	22	34	19	2	0	115.78
LJ Wright	not out	1	8	3	0	0	33.33
Extras	(lb 3, w 6)	9					
Total	(6 wickets; 50 overs; 212 mins)	229	(4.58 runs per over)				

Did not bat TT Bresnan, JC Tredwell, CT Tremlett
Fall of wickets 1-29 (Strauss, 7.6 ov), 2-31 (Bell, 8.6 ov), 3-95 (Bopara, 26.6 ov), 4-186 (Morgan, 42.6 ov), 5-186 (Swann, 43.1 ov), 6-212 (Trott, 48.3 ov)

Bowling	O	M	R	W	Econ	
SL Malinga	10	0	46	1	4.60	(2w)
TM Dilshan	6	1	25	1	4.16	(1w)
AD Mathews	5	0	20	1	4.00	
HMRKB Herath	10	1	47	0	4.70	
BAW Mendis	10	0	34	1	3.40	
M Muralitharan	9	0	54	2	6.00	(1w)

Sri Lanka innings		R	M	B	4s	6s	SR
WU Tharanga	not out	102	175	122	12	1	83.60
TM Dilshan	not out	108	175	115	10	2	93.91
Extras	(b 9, lb 6, w 6)	21					
Total	(0 wickets; 39.3 overs; 175 mins)	231	(5.84 runs per over)				

Did not bat KC Sangakkara*†, DPMD Jayawardene, TT Samaraweera, LPC Silva, AD Mathews, SL Malinga, HMRKB Herath, BAW Mendis, M Muralitharan

Bowling	O	M	R	W	Econ	
TT Bresnan	8	1	40	0	5.00	
GP Swann	9	0	61	0	6.77	(2w)
CT Tremlett	7.3	0	38	0	5.06	(1w)
RS Bopara	5	1	22	0	4.40	
JC Tredwell	6	0	38	0	6.33	
LJ Wright	4	0	17	0	4.25	(1w)

Sri Lanka won by 10 wickets (with 63 balls remaining)
Man of the match TM Dilshan (Sri Lanka)

Sri Lanka vs. New Zealand
29 March
R Premadasa Stadium, Colombo
Toss New Zealand chose to bat
Umpires Aleem Dar (Pakistan) and SJ Davis (Australia)

New Zealand innings		R	M	B	4s	6s	SR
MJ Guptill	b Malinga	39	91	65	3	0	60.00
BB McCullum†	b Herath	13	27	21	1	1	61.90
JD Ryder	c †Sangakkara b Muralitharan	19	48	34	2	0	55.88
LRPL Taylor	c Tharanga b Mendis	36	90	55	1	0	65.45
SB Styris	lbw b Muralitharan	57	119	77	5	0	74.02
KS Williamson	lbw b Malinga	22	23	16	3	0	137.50
NL McCullum	c †Sangakkara b Malinga	9	9	9	0	1	100.00
JDP Oram	c Jayawardene b Dilshan	7	14	9	1	0	77.77
DL Vettori*	not out	3	10	3	0	0	100.00
TG Southee	c †Sangakkara b Mendis	0	3	3	0	0	0.00
AJ McKay	b Mendis	0	1	2	0	0	0.00
Extras	(lb 5, w 6, nb 1)	12					
Total	(all out; 48.5 overs; 222 mins)	217	(4.44 runs per over)				

Fall of wickets 1-32 (BB McCullum, 7.1 ov), 2-69 (Ryder, 18.3 ov), 3-84 (Guptill, 21.3 ov), 4-161 (Taylor, 39.1 ov), 5-192 (Williamson, 43.3 ov), 6-204 (NL McCullum, 45.1 ov), 7-213 (Styris, 46.6 ov), 8-215 (Oram, 47.4 ov), 9-217 (Southee, 48.3 ov), 10-217 (McKay, 48.5 ov)

Bowling	O	M	R	W	Econ	
SL Malinga	9	0	55	3	6.11	(1nb)
HMRKB Herath	9	1	31	1	3.44	(1w)
AD Mathews	6	0	27	0	4.50	
BAW Mendis	9.5	0	35	3	3.55	
M Muralitharan	10	1	42	2	4.20	(2w)
TM Dilshan	5	0	22	1	4.40	(1w)

Sri Lanka innings		R	M	B	4s	6s	SR
WU Tharanga	c Ryder b Southee	30	29	31	4	1	96.77
TM Dilshan	c Ryder b Southee	73	142	93	10	1	78.49
KC Sangakkara*†	c Styris b McKay	54	132	79	7	1	68.35
DPMD Jayawardene	lbw b Vettori	1	3	3	0	0	33.33
TT Samaraweera	not out	23	77	38	2	0	60.52
LPC Silva	b Southee	13	29	25	2	0	52.00
AD Mathews	not out	14	31	18	1	1	77.77
Extras	(lb 2, w 10)	12					
Total	(5 wickets; 47.5 overs; 223 mins)	220	(4.59 runs per over)				

Did not bat SL Malinga, HMRKB Herath, BAW Mendis, M Muralitharan
Fall of wickets 1-40 (Tharanga, 7.2 ov), 2-160 (Dilshan, 32.4 ov), 3-161 (Jayawardene, 33.1 ov), 4-169 (Sangakkara, 36.2 ov), 5-185 (Silva, 42.2 ov)

Bowling	O	M	R	W	Econ	
NL McCullum	6	0	33	0	5.50	(1w)
TG Southee	10	2	57	3	5.70	(1w)
DL Vettori	10	0	36	1	3.60	
JDP Oram	8	1	29	0	3.62	
AJ McKay	9.5	1	37	1	3.76	(2w)
SB Styris	2	0	12	0	6.00	
JD Ryder	2	0	14	0	7.00	

Sri Lanka won by 5 wickets (with 13 balls remaining)
Man of the match KC Sangakkara (Sri Lanka)

India v Pakistan

30 March
Punjab Cricket Association Stadium, Mohali, Chandigarh
Toss India chose to bat
Umpires IJ Gould (England) and SJA Taufel (Australia)

India innings		R	M	B	4s	6s	SR
V Sehwag	lbw b Wahab Riaz	38	32	25	9	0	152.00
SR Tendulkar	c Shahid Afridi b Saeed Ajmal	85	160	115	11	0	73.91
G Gambhir	st †Kamran Akmal b Mohammad Hafeez	27	55	32	2	0	84.37
V Kohli	c Umar Akmal b Wahab Riaz	9	20	21	0	0	42.85
Yuvraj Singh	b Wahab Riaz	0	1	1	0	0	0.00
MS Dhoni*†	lbw b Wahab Riaz	25	64	42	2	0	59.52
SK Raina	not out	36	69	39	3	0	92.30
Harbhajan Singh	st †Kamran Akmal b Saeed Ajmal	12	28	15	2	0	80.00
Z Khan	c †Kamran Akmal b Wahab Riaz	9	14	10	1	0	90.00
A Nehra	run out (Wahab Riaz/†Kamran Akmal)	1	1	2	0	0	50.00
MM Patel	not out	0	1	0	0	0	–
Extras	(lb 8, w 8, nb 2)	18					
Total	(9 wickets; 50 overs; 231 mins)	260	(5.20 runs per over)				

Fall of wickets 1-48 (Sehwag, 5.5 ov), 2-116 (Gambhir, 18.5 ov), 3-141 (Kohli, 25.2 ov), 4-141 (Yuvraj Singh, 25.3 ov), 5-187 (Tendulkar, 36.6 ov), 6-205 (Dhoni, 41.4 ov), 7-236 (Harbhajan Singh, 46.4 ov), 8-256 (Khan, 49.2 ov), 9-258 (Nehra, 49.5 ov)

Bowling	O	M	R	W	Econ	
Umar Gul	8	0	69	0	8.62	(2nb, 1w)
Abdul Razzaq	2	0	14	0	7.00	
Wahab Riaz	10	0	46	5	4.60	(4w)
Saeed Ajmal	10	0	44	2	4.40	(2w)
Shahid Afridi	10	0	45	0	4.50	
Mohammad Hafeez	10	0	34	1	3.40	

Pakistan innings		R	M	B	4s	6s	SR
Kamran Akmal†	c Yuvraj Singh b Khan	19	40	21	3	0	90.47
Mohammad Hafeez	c †Dhoni b Patel	43	66	59	7	0	72.88
Asad Shafiq	b Yuvraj Singh	30	61	39	2	0	76.92
Younis Khan	c Raina b Yuvraj Singh	13	44	32	0	0	40.62
Misbah-ul-Haq	c Kohli b Khan	56	134	76	5	1	73.68
Umar Akmal	b Harbhajan Singh	29	35	24	1	2	120.83
Abdul Razzaq	b Patel	3	12	9	0	0	33.33
Shahid Afridi*	c Sehwag b Harbhajan Singh	19	25	17	1	0	111.76
Wahab Riaz	c Tendulkar b Nehra	8	16	14	1	0	57.14
Umar Gul	lbw b Nehra	2	9	3	0	0	66.66
Saeed Ajmal	not out	1	18	5	0	0	20.00
Extras	(w 8)	8					
Total	(all out; 49.5 overs; 239 mins)	231	(4.63 runs per over)				

Fall of wickets 1-44 (Kamran Akmal, 8.6 ov), 2-70 (Mohammad Hafeez, 15.3 ov), 3-103 (Asad Shafiq, 23.5 ov), 4-106 (Younis Khan, 25.4 ov), 5-142 (Umar Akmal, 33.1 ov), 6-150 (Abdul Razzaq, 36.2 ov), 7-184 (Shahid Afridi, 41.5 ov), 8-199 (Wahab Riaz, 44.5 ov), 9-208 (Umar Gul, 46.1 ov), 10-231 (Misbah-ul-Haq, 49.5 ov)

Bowling	O	M	R	W	Econ	
Z Khan	9.5	0	58	2	5.89	(2w)
A Nehra	10	0	33	2	3.30	(1w)
MM Patel	10	1	40	2	4.00	(1w)
Harbhajan Singh	10	0	43	2	4.30	
Yuvraj Singh	10	1	57	2	5.70	

India won by 29 runs
Man of the match SR Tendulkar (India)

India vs. Sri Lanka
2 April
Wankhede Stadium, Mumbai
Toss Sri Lanka chose to bat
Umpires Aleem Dar (Pakistan) and SJA Taufel (Australia)

Sri Lanka innings		R	M	B	4s	6s	SR
WU Tharanga	c Sehwag b Khan	2	30	20	0	0	10.00
TM Dilshan	b Harbhajan Singh	33	87	49	3	0	67.34
KC Sangakkara*†	c †Dhoni b Yuvraj Singh	48	102	67	5	0	71.64
DPMD Jayawardene	not out	103	159	88	13	0	117.04
TT Samaraweera	lbw b Yuvraj Singh	21	53	34	2	0	61.76
CK Kapugedera	c Raina b Khan	1	6	5	0	0	20.00
KMDN Kulasekara	run out (†Dhoni)	32	41	30	1	1	106.66
NLTC Perera	not out	22	10	9	3	1	244.44
Extras	(b 1, lb 3, w 6, nb 2)	12					
Total	(6 wickets; 50 overs; 246 mins)	274	(5.48 runs per over)				

Did not bat SL Malinga, S Randiv, M Muralitharan
Fall of wickets 1-17 (Tharanga, 6.1 ov), 2-60 (Dilshan, 16.3 ov), 3-122 (Sangakkara, 27.5 ov), 4-179 (Samaraweera, 38.1 ov), 5-182 (Kapugedera, 39.5 ov), 6-248 (Kulasekara, 47.6 ov)

Bowling	O	M	R	W	Econ	
Z Khan	10	3	60	2	6.00	(1w)
S Sreesanth	8	0	52	0	6.50	(2nb)
MM Patel	9	0	41	0	4.55	(1w)
Harbhajan Singh	10	0	50	1	5.00	(1w)
Yuvraj Singh	10	0	49	2	4.90	
SR Tendulkar	2	0	12	0	6.00	(3w)
V Kohli	1	0	6	0	6.00	

India innings		R	M	B	4s	6s	SR
V Sehwag	lbw b Malinga	0	2	2	0	0	0.00
SR Tendulkar	c †Sangakkara b Malinga	18	21	14	2	0	128.57
G Gambhir	b Perera	97	187	122	9	0	79.50
V Kohli	c & b Dilshan	35	69	49	4	0	71.42
MS Dhoni*†	not out	91	128	79	8	2	115.18
Yuvraj Singh	not out	21	39	24	2	0	87.50
Extras	(b 1, lb 6, w 8)	15					
Total	(4 wickets; 48.2 overs; 230 mins)	277	(5.73 runs per over)				

Did not bat SK Raina, Harbhajan Singh, Z Khan, MM Patel, S Sreesanth
Fall of wickets 1-0 (Sehwag, 0.2 ov), 2-31 (Tendulkar, 6.1 ov), 3-114 (Kohli, 21.4 ov), 4-223 (Gambhir, 41.2 ov)

Bowling	O	M	R	W	Econ	
SL Malinga	9	0	42	2	4.66	(2w)
KMDN Kulasekara	8.2	0	64	0	7.68	
NLTC Perera	9	0	55	1	6.11	(2w)
S Randiv	9	0	43	0	4.77	
TM Dilshan	5	0	27	1	5.40	(1w)
M Muralitharan	8	0	39	0	4.87	(1w)

India won by 6 wickets (with 10 balls remaining)
Man of the match MS Dhoni (India)
Player of the tournament Yuvraj Singh (India)

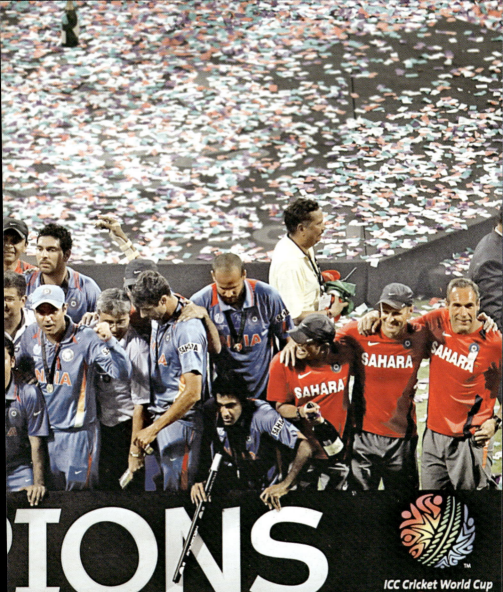

ACKNOWLEDGEMENTS

Soon after the World Cup ended, I had a call from V.K. Karthika, publisher of HarperCollins India. The gist of our conversation was:

Karthika: 'How about it?'

Self: 'Of course.'

And that's how this book was born. Karthika, whose fertile mind is always on red alert, deserves full credit for putting it together in a remarkably short time. I cannot thank her enough for her initiative, enthusiasm, sheer hard work and ready laughter. She is the best friend a writer can have. Thanks to Shuka Jain and Anuj Malhotra who translated the ideas into this book.

I owe a debt of gratitude to friends and colleagues Sambit Bal of Cricinfo, Tarun Tejpal of *Tehelka*, Nirmal Sekhar and Shalini Arun of *The Hindu*, Vijay Tagore of *DNA*, G. Raghunath of *Sportstar*, Ayanjit Sen and Rajarshi Gupta of ESPN, Venu Palaparthi and Atul Huckoo of Dreamcricket, K.O Paulson of *Saudi Gazette*. Special thanks to my favourite cricket-watching and cricket-talking buddies Ramachandra Guha, Bishan Bedi, Vedam Jaishankar, Makarand Waigankar, Peter Roebuck, who were also companions in the journey that was the World Cup.

Finally, as always, for believing that staring out the window is a crucial part of my research, my wife Dimpy and son Tushar who make it all seem worthwhile.

Apart from the newspapers, magazines and websites mentioned above, I have also consulted *Wisden Cricketers' Almanack, The Guardian, Daily Telegraph, The Independent, Times of India, Indian Express, Sydney Morning Herald, The Age*, and the following books: *A Corner of a Foreign Field* by Ramachandra Guha, *Silent Revolutions* by Gideon Haigh, *A Century of Great Cricket Quotes* by David Hopps, *Pundits from Pakistan* by Rahul Bhattacharya, *Cricket Wallah* by Scyld Berry and *In It to Win It* by Peter Roebuck.